CHICKEN
SHACK

GROWING UP BLACK AND POOR IN ALABAMA
DURING THE 1940'S, 50'S AND 60'S

An inspirational and motivational exposé
on survival, fortitude and perseverance

JOE NATHAN HILL

Fulton Books, Inc.
Meadville, PA

Published by Fulton Books 2016

ISBN 978-1-63338-244-2 (Paperback)
ISBN 978-1-63338-245-9 (Digital)

Printed in the United States of America

Contents

Dedication

I dedicate this book to my deceased parents who instilled in my siblings and me the value of getting a good education and having the fortitude, courage, and perseverance to achieve our goals and to always do our best. Unfortunately, neither of them—due to dire economic circumstances, systemic racism, segregation and discrimination—had an opportunity to get a good education themselves or earn a good living. My father quit school in the first grade. Therefore, he never learned to read or write. My mother received the equivalent of a sixth grade education. The school she attended was a two-room wooden structure that was built with funds contributed by the Southern Aid Society through the Freedman's Bureau. At an early age, in Lowndes County, Alabama, where my parents grew up, they were engaged in planting and harvesting crops on farms owned by whites. This was necessary as a means of survival. Lowndes County was mostly agricultural and heavily populated with unskilled blacks who outnumbered whites approximately four to one.

In July 1968, at age fifty-eight, my father died of heart disease. Due to my parents' meager income and my father's relatively early demise, my parents, as a couple, never had an opportunity to enjoy some of the simple pleasures in life. For example, they never went to the movies together, took a trip on a bus, train, or an airplane; they never dined at a classy restaurant, stayed overnight in a classy hotel, vacationed on the beach, or went on a cruise. My father died about four years after passage of the 1964 Civil Rights Act (CRA). The CRA was a very significant piece of civil rights legislation that had far-reaching socioeconomic effects in its implementation and effectuation. Unfortunately, my father didn't live long enough to fully perceive the stupendous impact the CRA had in creating employment and educational opportunities for blacks.

My mother lived to be age ninety-six. Because of her longevity, she witnessed countless life-changing opportunities that the CRA created for blacks and other minorities. She witnessed many changes that occurred in social, economic, and political realms that were unprecedented. These changes significantly improved the socioeconomic and sociopolitical status of many blacks. The Voting Rights Act of 1965 was also a major piece of civil rights legislation. Finally, blacks without hindrance had an opportunity to participate in the political election process and their votes without question, past and present, vastly influenced the results of many elections. My mother, without hesitation, eagerly availed herself of privileges afforded blacks that were a direct result of the CRA and the Voting Rights Act. In April 2007, my mother passed away. Prior to her death she was diagnosed with colon cancer.

This writing is also dedicated to all the families that lived in the neighborhood (Greater Washington Park) where I grew up. Like my family, these families had to continually deal with racial prejudice, segregation, and discrimination that were promulgated by a white supremacy ideology entrenched in the psyche of many white Alabamians. Furthermore, like my family, they also had to continually deal with economic difficulties and financial hardships that existed primarily because we were black and didn't have any or very limited employment options or avenues to improve our lot.

School my mother attended

Preface

The bus boycott in Montgomery, Alabama, in 1955, the congressional Civil Rights Act of 1964, and certain court cases had a tremendous impact on the lives of blacks in bringing about positive changes socially, economically, politically, and educationally. Many things changed for the better.

The standard of living and overall living conditions for young blacks today are a lot different than they were when I grew up in rural and rurban parts of Alabama over six decades ago. Today, the vast majority of black youths in Alabama, including those who live in rural and rurban areas as I did, live in houses or apartments that have electricity, natural gas, running water, central heat and air. Most of them have their individual bed to sleep in and don't have to share with a sibling. Their houses or apartments are equipped with gas or electric stoves to cook their food, not to mention microwave ovens. They don't have to be concerned about eating certain foods as quickly as possible before they spoil because they have refrigerators/freezers to keep them fresh. Their houses or apartments have hot and cold running water readily available so they can a take a shower or a bath as often as they like. They don't have to wait for a sunny day to wash their clothes so they can hang them outside to dry. Their clothes are washed and dried in a matter of minutes because they have immediate access to electric washers and dryers. Most of them eat three meals a day, plus snacks and have a large variety of foods from which to choose.

Many have a large array of fashionable clothes, several pair of shoes, and a huge selection of electronic games and toys. Additionally, they have cable ready color televisions, the internet via desktop, laptop, handheld computers, and other wireless computerized electronic devices for educational, communicative, and entertainment purposes. To stay in touch with family and friends, they have highly sophisticated cell phones with text-messaging capability and other high-tech features. Some drive cars that many gainfully employed adults can't afford.

Different than when I was in public elementary, middle, and high school, textbooks nowadays are free, and most black students attend schools that are much more environmentally comfortable and conducive to learning. School buildings are aesthetically beautiful inside and out, architecturally attractive, and structurally sound. Generally, schools today have state-of-the-art educational materials and equipment that are designed to facilitate learning. Yet we continue to have students fail academically and/or drop out of school. Maybe we as parents and grandparents in continual collaboration with teachers and guidance counselors need to be more proactive and aggressive in identifying why a student is failing or drops out of school. Once the cause is determined, we should take positive steps as quickly as possible to remedy the situation. If the student needs academic help, the responsible staff person or school official should promptly refer the student to the appropriate source for tutorial help; if there is a self-esteem, emotional, or psychological issue or family crisis, the student and/or parent(s) should be promptly referred for professional medical help. Sometimes, encouraging and motivating the student and just showing that somebody cares is all it takes to keep the student focused and on track academically.

During the civil rights movement, a number of individuals, black and white, lost their lives in the fight for "equal rights" for blacks. For this reason alone, blacks have a moral obligation to strive with unparalleled fervor and enthusiasm to be all that they can be or to achieve all that they can achieve. It is heartbreaking to see black youths drop out of school year after year, seemingly having no desire or motivation to go to school and get a good education. Unfortunately, a significant number of these students have the potential for greatness and high achievement that they may never have an opportunity to demonstrate. This is such a waste of talent and ability. Initiatives such as the No Child Left Behind program, an increased emphasis on parental and community involvement, and youth-services organizations have had a positive impact, but we are still losing too many young blacks to gangs, the streets, and prison. Maybe divine guidance is the answer. God loves each of us individually and wants us to accept Him as our Savior and seek His guidance.

I'm glad God loves us. His love is incomparable and unconditional. What an awesome and almighty God He is! He is almighty because He is omnipotent (has unlimited power), omniscient (has unlimited knowledge), omnipresent (present in all places at all times), and "omnicompetent" (able to handle any situation). Also, I'm glad we are all God's children. Because we are His children, He wants each of us to be happy, have a good life, and prosper. So remember that God is pleased when His children are happy, healthy, and prosperous. Prayerfully, this treatise will be a positive source of inspiration, motivation, and encouragement for you as you pursue your dreams and ambitions.

Introduction

I have prepared this exposé to share what life was like for my family and me living in rural, rurban, and urban Alabama during the 1940s, '50s, and '60s. Life for my family, a poor black family, living in Alabama during these decades was quite challenging. Even more challenging was being a poor black male growing up in Alabama during the '40s, '50s, and '60s. I am hopeful and optimistic that this document convincingly and persuasively sends the message that you can succeed if you are determined and if you remain steadfast in pursuit of your dreams and ambitions in spite of fluctuant changes in your social, economic, or financial status. I know from experience that financially, things can get to a point where there seems to be no way out. Don't give up on your dreams. Refuse to be defeated. In my constant struggle to survive and achieve my goals, life was in no way easy.

Based on my experiences in achieving my goals, I've developed the following archetype of a road to success. It's only a model. If you use it, I sincerely believe you as well will achieve success.

DETERMINATION: ONE OF SEVERAL ROADS TO SUCCESS

A road that leads to success one might want to travel is called determination. It branches out into thirteen essential streets that intersect four essential avenues. The four avenues are fortitude, perseverance, resilience, and flexibility". These avenues and the thirteen intersecting streets listed below help you successfully manage challenging obstacles such as potholes, soft shoulders, sharp curves, steep hills, drop-offs, pileups, and slippery surfaces. They also help you successfully manage and recover from unexpected roadblocks, traffic jams, and detours. No matter how often traveled and by whom, these four avenues and thirteen streets will ultimately take you to *success*. The thirteen streets that branch out from the road of determination are

(1) Drive
  (2) Enthusiasm
    (3) Tenacity
      (4) Endurance
        (5) Resourcefulness
          (6) Maturity
            (7) Ingenuity
              (8) Navigation
                (9) Attentiveness
                  (10) Temperance
                    (11) Initiative
                      (12) Organization
                        (13) Negotiation

When I reflect on the financial vicissitudes, the oppressive economic realities, and the distressed environmental conditions my family and I faced, I find it astonishingly amazing that we were able to maintain the mental and physical tenacity we needed to persevere. Making life even more difficult was the preponderance of racism, segregation, and discrimination. With this said, let this writing serve as a reminder to everyone that it benefits all of us when we can live, study, play and work together in harmony without regard to race, color, gender, sexual orientation, or religion.

While this exposé is primarily designed to inspire and motivate, it is also designed to enlighten and educate. Prayerfully, it will be of value to all segments of the population, especially middle and high school students. Life for many individuals today is just as challenging economically and financially as it was for my family and me during the '40s, '50s, and '60s. Many children and adults today go to bed hungry every night and wake up hungry every morning, not knowing from where their next meal is coming. Unfortunately, many of these children and adults are homeless individuals living on the streets. A few lucky ones live in shelters. So let us be mindful that as we receive financial and other blessings, we should in turn bless someone by sharing our good fortune. Remember, there are many individuals, some we know and some we don't, who need someone to care enough to help in a tangible or intangible way.

I enjoy reading the words in songs found in old hymnals. I've found that many of the songs contain inspiring and uplifting verse that's relevant to situations and circumstances that many of us deal with on a daily basis. Therefore, as you read this book, you will find several excerpts from some of the songs.

Heritage

My father was born in Hayneville, Alabama, in 1909. Hayneville is the county seat of Lowndes County and is situated in the central part of the county. In the early 1900s, Hayneville had a population of six hundred. It had a small cottonseed mill, cotton gin, a grits mill, and a sawmill. Hayneville's population today (2016) is approximately 587.

My father's father presumably was white. His mother was multiracial (white-black-Chinese). My father was the elder of seven siblings, six boys and one girl (fifth sibling). The second, third, and fourth brothers also had white fathers. The fifth sibling had a biracial (white-black) father. The father of the sixth and seventh siblings was black of African descent only. The four siblings with white fathers had different fathers. This exemplifies and is a good example of how the white male took advantage of the poor black female prior to desegregation.

Distinguishing racial characteristics of my father and his siblings were heavily manifested in the pigmentation in their skin and other physical features. The siblings who had white fathers had a very light complexion and a facial bone structure that strongly resembled the white race. The one with a biracial father was light-brown skinned and had facial features reflecting the white heritage but less pronounced. The two brothers who had a black father (of African descent only) were very dark skinned and had facial features more reflective of the African race but less pronounced. My father, the second, third, and fourth brothers could easily have passed for white.

My father's mother couldn't read or write. To have some income, she did laundry for several white families in the Hayneville area. Being black, poor, unskilled, uneducated, and bereft of a sustainable steady income to support her children, my father's mother was at an economic disadvantage and was quite vulnerable to psychological and sexual exploitation by the opposite sex. Consequently, she was emotionally and sexually involved with several men who weren't serious about having a lasting male–female relationship. Neither of them was meaningfully involved in her life for any significant length of time.

Of the seven siblings, the second brother escaped the distress of growing up in Hayneville, where economic hardship seemed to have been a perpetual way of life for poor blacks. He was exceptionally lucky. He was one of a few biracial children that the white father substantially provided financial support. His father arranged for him to attend a Catholic boarding school in Florida where he received his high school diploma. When he graduated, he went to Detroit, Michigan, to live with a close relative of his father. At age twenty, he went to work for General Motors, Chrysler division. He worked for Chrysler for thirty-five years. When he retired, he was a supervisor. I'm sure he passed for white while he worked for Chrysler. He had two sons. They are both deceased.

The third brother never moved from Hayneville and, like my father, never attended school and couldn't read or write. He worked at the local white high school as a janitor. In his early sixties, he became totally blind and could no longer work. He had seven daughters. Three of them are deceased.

The fourth brother lived in Hayneville until his early teens. He married at an early age and moved to Cincinnati, Ohio. Fortunately, his wife had an uncle who lived in Cincinnati who was in the army and able to provide a place for them to live until he found a job. He found a job at a foundry, where he worked until he retired. Even though he attended school for a short while, he too received a very limited education. However, his children taught him how to write his name. He had four girls and two boys. One girl is deceased.

The fifth and sixth brothers served in the military (the US Army). Neither of them finished high school. When they were discharged from the army, the fifth brother moved to Chicago, Illinois, where he worked as a mechanic. He had two boys and a girl. The sixth brother made his home in Cleveland, Ohio. He was employed at a manufacturing plant and also worked part time at a dry cleaner. He had four children, three girls and a boy.

My dad's sister was the second of the siblings to get a high school diploma. Upon graduating from high school, she moved to Cleveland, Ohio, where she met her husband and continued to live there until his death. She was living in Cleveland when the sixth brother moved there from Alabama. She went to school to be a beautician and worked at a white beauty shop as the shampoo person until she retired. She also worked part time with her brother at the dry cleaner. She was the only sibling who didn't have children. When her husband died, she returned to Hayneville to live and to take care of her mother. After her mother died, she continued to live in Hayneville until her death about two years prior to the baby brother's death.

My father and all of his siblings are deceased. My father was the first of the siblings to pass away. The seventh and youngest sibling (my uncle who lived in Cleveland) was the last one to die.

When my father and his siblings were growing up, they didn't have a constant father figure in their lives. Their mother never married. My dad's mother told him a white man for whom she washed and ironed shirts was his father. Apparently, she was his mistress. Since this man already had a family of his own, for obvious reasons, he never openly acknowledged my father as his son. Therefore, my father only knew of him and never had a father–son relationship with him. Because my father was born at a time when racism and segregation were prevalent, there was never any intercommunication or interaction between them. Things were kept quiet because of fear of reprisal.

Before my father was born, his mother also had an intimate and sexual relationship with a biracial black man. To save face and to give my father a sense of belonging, she told friends and neighbors this man was my dad's father. Consequently, my father had a presumed white father and a presumed black father. My dad didn't have a father–son relationship with the black father either, and there was no interaction or any form of communication between them. Apparently, having a sense of belonging was very important to my father because he accepted the black man as his father and became very close to one of his half-brothers. They did a lot of hunting and fishing together and would frequently visit each other at their homes.

In Lowndes County, during the decade my father was born and the decade that followed, an appreciable number of poor black females bore children out of wedlock for white males. An open miscegenational relationship between a white male and a black female, as far as whites were concerned, was unacceptable. However, sexual intercourse between the white male and black female was a common occurrence that was routinely accepted and generally ignored by most blacks. Many of the children that were born as a result of these casual relationships never received from the father sufficient monetary or material support such as food, shoes or clothes. My dad was one of those. Neither did my father receive any type of support from his presumed black father. As a result of the lack of paternal support, he had to help support himself the best he could.

My father, who was quite young, went to work at age six as a day laborer picking cotton, gathering sweet potatoes, pulling corn. and doing whatever menial work he could find. As he grew older, he found steady work for a white doctor and his family that lived in the area. He took on a lot of responsibility trying to help provide for himself, his mother, and younger siblings. Since he dropped out of school and began to work at age six, he didn't have an opportunity to go to school and learn the three fundamental educational skills (reading, writing, and arithmetic (the three r's) that were necessary for him to grow intellectually and be able to compete for jobs. In Hayneville though, I'm sure any jobs requiring these skills were either extremely limited or nonexistent for black males.

My father never personally knew his paternal or maternal grandparents. Because his presumed white father never acknowledged him as his son and races were segregated, my father didn't have an opportunity to get to know his white father's parents. In the midst of segregation and my father's chaotic family situation, I'm not sure he had a desire to get to know his white father's parents or if it really mattered. To my knowledge, the issue of his white paternal grandparents' anonymity was seldom mentioned or discussed. Unfortunately, my father didn't have a relationship with his presumed black paternal grandparents either.

Regarding my father's maternal grandparents, if his mother shared information or discussed things about them with him other than their race, he never enlightened my siblings or me. His mother's father was biracial (white-Chinese), and his mother's mother was also biracial (white-black). The only thing he shared with us about his mother's family was that they lived in South Carolina. Evidently, his mother came to Alabama from South Carolina, and she came without her parents.

To learn more about my paternal grandmother, I checked the 1900, 1910, the 1920 census records. Consequently, I found that she had a brother who was six years younger than her and that they both lived in a boarding house in 1900. When I checked the 1910 Census Records, I didn't find any information on her brother. It appeared that he just vanished. Evidently, my father didn't know about his uncle because he never mentioned him. It's a wonderment to know that I have close black and Chinese cousins on my grandmother's paternal side of the family and close white and black relatives on her maternal side of the family. Regrettably, I don't have the genealogy information I need to do a thorough genealogical search.

My mother was born in Lowndesboro, Alabama, in 1911. Like Hayneville, Lowndesboro is a small town in Lowndes County and in the early 1900s had a population of 400. It is located about twelve miles northeast of Hayneville. Lowndesboro's population today (2016) is approximately 111.

My mother's father was black (African heritage only), and her mother was part black (African heritage only) and Creek Indian. My mother was the second of four girls. Her complexion and her youngest sister's complexion was dark like their father's. The two other sisters had skin color that was medium brown, more closely resembling their mother's. All of my mother's sisters preceded her in death. None of her sisters finished high school. Her elder sister lived on a farm in Selma, Alabama, and her livelihood in part depended a lot on the money she earned working in cotton and cornfields. She had two sons and a daughter who are all deceased.

The third sister lived in Montgomery, Alabama, and was employed at an automobile upholstery and seat cover company. She also worked as a beautician for several years. She had two boys and a girl. The elder son is deceased. My mother's youngest sister was the first to die. She also lived in Montgomery, where she worked as a presser at a dry cleaner on Maxwell Air Force Base and at a privately owned dry cleaner in the neighborhood where she lived. She had three sons and a daughter who are all deceased.

Even though my mother's father didn't spend much time with her and her siblings, they did see him often enough to get to know him. However, he was not a stable force in their lives. He was in and out of the household a lot and provided very little financial support. He was a guitar player and blues singer. To earn some money, he frequently performed at juke joints and house parties. When I saw him for the first time, my family was living in Montgomery. The first thing I noticed about him was that he had one leg. The right leg had been amputated above the knee. I asked my mother what happened. She said she was told he worked at the sawmill in Hayneville when he was young and his leg got caught in the lumber conveyor. She didn't seem to know much about his personal life or him as an individual. What she knew was mostly hearsay. She was told he had five different sets of children and had never been married. Apparently, he was a womanizer. I wonder if he really lost his leg in an accident at the sawmill.

Like my father and his siblings, my mother and her siblings didn't get much financial support from their father neither. And also like my father, they worked in cotton, corn, and sweet potato fields to earn some money. Fortunately, my mother managed to go to school and complete the sixth grade. Because blacks had to work in the aforementioned fields during peak cultivation, planting, and harvesting months, schools for blacks were in session only six months.

My mother dropped out of school after the sixth grade. She dropped out because the older she got, the more responsibility she assumed in ensuring that her personal needs were met, such as buying clothes and shoes.

Unlike my father, my mother knew her paternal and maternal grandparents. Her father's parents were African. Her mother's father was black, and her mother's mother was Creek Indian. My mother spent a lot of time with her mother's parents and had a good relationship with them. She would occasionally speak of them and say some good things about them, like how nurturing and caring they were and how close they were as a family. She didn't spend as much time with her father's parents. When she mentioned them, she mostly talked about her grandfather and how industrious he was.

Based on the conversations she had with my siblings and me, she didn't spend much time with her paternal grandmother. She never explained why. Hence, I've come to the conclusion that this was because her father never spent much quality time with her and her sisters. Apparently, my mother's father seldom took her and her siblings to visit with his parents for any extended length of time. Fortunately though, I know many close relatives on both my mother's maternal and paternal sides of the family.

My father and mother were physically attractive individuals. My father had a medium build and was about five feet nine inches tall. His hair was straight and fine in texture. My mother was slender and about five feet three inches tall. Her hair was long, wavy, and coarse. As a couple, they nicely complemented each other in terms of physical appearance.

My mother and father

Considering my parent's personalities, my father was low-key, soft spoken, and easygoing. He was not a "rock the boat" kind of person. He would usually go with the flow and had an "If it's not broken don't fix it" attitude. However, if he was provoked and became really incensed, he could be explosive. He was devoted to his work. He was loyal, punctual, and believed in doing an excellent job. Whereas, my father was low-key and soft spoken, my mother was not. Maybe this is why they got along so well when they married. My mother was very vocal, proactive, assertive, and outgoing. She wasn't afraid to "rock the boat" especially if she believed she was right.

Based on some things my mother and father told my siblings and me, it appears my mother may have had an innate boldness that was God given. She was daring and not easily intimidated by anybody, white or black. She didn't condone violence and, to my knowledge, never instigated any violent acts. She was very intuitive and perceptive. There was something special about her. It seemed she had this amazing ability to identify a business opportunity and act on it. Her action usually resulted in a successful business venture with a profitable outcome. She was continually optimistic and never let a problem or concern get the best of her. She was a positive thinker and believed in God and the power of prayer. Over the years, many times I heard her say, "Trust in God," "The Lord will make a way," "The Lord will provide," "God knows best," and "God doesn't make mistakes." She had a lot of ingenuity and was also quite resourceful. If she had been fortunate enough to complete her education and had the necessary resources, I believe she could have been a very successful entrepreneur.

Although my parents had quite different personalities, sociably and recreationally they both had two things in common: they were generous individuals, and they enjoyed using tobacco products. They were always ready to share with others any food they had and any material items such as farm equipment, lawn, and gardening tools. If there was something they could do to help someone in some way, they were always willing. My father chewed Brown Mule sweet chewing tobacco and occasionally smoked cigars. In choosing cigars to smoke, he usually smoked the cheapest he could buy.

Regarding chewing tobacco, I had an unpleasant experience that I would like to share with you. For several years, I observed my father and some of his friends enjoy chewing tobacco, especially when we were standing around talking before we went coon hunting. The big wad of tobacco inside the mouth pressing against the cheek, the spitting, and the tobacco juice dripping from both sides of the mouth was something to see. Man! It appeared that chewing tobacco was so much fun. Being the adventurous person that I am, I decided that if chewing tobacco was that much fun, I had to try it.

So one Saturday afternoon when my father and I were outside working in the yard, I begged him to give me a piece of his tobacco to chew. I was age twelve. He tried to discourage me, but I was very persistent. Finally, he gave me a piece and cautioned me not to swallow any of the juice. I was happy. While chewing the tobacco, I could taste the sweet flavor of it and savored the sweetness of the juice it made as it mixed with my saliva. Oops! I swallowed some of the juice. In a few seconds, my head was spinning. I was dizzy, and my heart was pounding. I had an excruciating headache and stomachache. I was nauseated and couldn't keep my physical equilibrium. So I simply fell to the ground. I cried out, "Lord, help me, I'm dying." I was too weak to stand up. My father, seemingly undisturbed about what was happening, calmly said, "You gonna be all right." I had to lie on the ground for about forty-five minutes until the dizziness passed. Almost as quickly as it started, my tobacco chewing ended.

My father continued to chew tobacco and occasionally smoked cigars until his death.

My mother dipped big S bitter snuff and smoked Winston cigarettes. My middle sister, curious like I was in my wanting to chew our dad's tobacco, decided she would dip some of our mother's snuff. However, she decided to secretly dip the snuff, and while doing so, she inadvertently swallowed some of the snuff. After swallowing the snuff, she got really dizzy and passed out. She gave our parents a serious scare. She lost consciousness for several hours, and our parents thought they needed to take her to the doctor when all of a sudden she regained consciousness and was physically okay.

I would occasionally smoke one of my mother's cigarettes or one of my dad's cigars but never took up the habit because I just didn't like the taste the smoke left in my mouth. My mother usually dipped snuff when she was sitting in a chair relaxing on the porch, working outside in the yard or in her vegetable gardens, or when she went fishing. She eventually stopped dipping snuff but continued to smoke cigarettes until she died.

Both Hayneville and Lowndesboro had their own business districts that included grocery shops and a post office. In 1865, Wilson's raiders marched on Lowndesboro, and it never returned to its original state. The business district burned in 1927, and none of the stores were rebuilt. On the weekends, blacks who lived in Lowndesboro would go to Hayneville or Montgomery to shop for groceries, clothes, and other goods. My mother went shopping in Hayneville one Saturday morning, and while she was walking down the street, like a magnet, she was uncontrollably drawn to this handsome young man coming in her direction. The attraction was so strong she couldn't take her eyes off of him. This handsome young man would later become my father. Using a very familiar cliché, it was love at first sight. They fell head over heels for each other.

A few months later in 1927 (my father was seventeen and my mother was sixteen) they indecorously exchanged wedding vows at the Hayneville courthouse. An older friend of theirs signed the necessary papers for them to get married. Their parents were surprised when they were apprised of the marriage. There was nothing they could do, and I'm thinking they were probably happy. As far as my mother was concerned, she and my dad were in love and they were meant to be together.

When my parents got married, the doctor for whom my father worked had taught him how to drive a Model T Ford, and he had become the doctor's chauffeur. The doctor enjoyed quail hunting. So he taught my father how to breed and train bird dogs. When he wasn't chauffeuring or training bird dogs, my father also worked for a white rancher and farmer who raised and sold beef cattle and quarter horses. This gentleman, for whom my dad's mom also did laundry, really liked my father as a worker and gave him a white stallion that he rode to and from work.

Before my parents decided to get married, they had already found a place to stay. They rented a small house located a few miles up the highway northeast of Hayneville. They lived there for several years. In the meantime, they tried to start a family, but my mother had two miscarriages, one in 1928 and one in 1931. In 1940, she had gynecological surgery (several fibroid tumors and an ovary removed) and thought she would never successfully have any children. Seemingly reconciled and content that this might be true, she continued to work as usual, picking cotton to earn some money. She was paid twenty-five cents for every hundred pounds she picked. She owned a Jersey milk cow and raised Rhode Island Red chickens. There was a pecan tree on the place they rented. To earn some extra money, she sold eggs and pecans. She also had a vegetable garden and she sold collard and turnip greens, okra, and tomatoes. Since she and my dad didn't have any children yet, they managed to save some money that would later provide them a wonderful opportunity.

An elderly biracial gentleman lived on a farm not very far from my parents. Because he was elderly, my parents would often help him with chores around the house and farm. Since he didn't have any children and the farm had gotten to be more than he could handle, he decided to move away to live with relatives. The white rancher for whom my dad worked for part-time was a good friend to this man's uncle. Because he liked my parents and knew they could use a nicer place, he decided to sell the place to them for much less than what it was worth. He thought of my parents as family. This was an unusual act of kindness. Farmland in the area sold for five dollars to forty dollars per acre.

The house on the property was a lot nicer and bigger than the house my mom and dad were renting. Even better, it had a pecan orchard (twelve pecan trees) and about twenty acres of land with a fenced pasture, pond, chicken yard, and hog pin. They knew they wanted to buy the place and would use the money they had saved, but they didn't have quite enough. There was one problem. Where were they going to get the additional money they needed? They decided they would talk the situation over with the doctor for whom my dad worked.

The doctor decided to lend them the money they needed, interest free, with the understanding that they would pay him a certain amount each month (I don't recall the exact amount, but I'm thinking five dollars a month). They signed a promissory note to this effect. Thinking ahead, they borrowed enough money so they didn't have to use all of the money they had saved when they bought the property. Therefore, they were able to buy several calves from the rancher for whom my father worked. This was a smart thing to do because they knew the investment would turn a nice profit when the calves matured and were sold. Since my parents didn't have any children yet, they paid more than what they owed each month and were able to pay off the promissory note in about two years and own the property outright.

When the word got out about what my parents had accomplished and how well they were doing financially, there were some very unhappy whites in the Hayneville area. The doctor for whom my father worked was called a nigger lover. This was an exceptionally desirable property, and the prevailing attitude of some whites in the area was that this property was too nice for my mom and dad to own. A friend of my parents came to their house late one night to inform them that he had heard some whites had gotten together and were planning to burn the house. In the meantime, the resentment and hostility perpetrated by whites escalated to acts of criminality in that some chickens and livestock were poisoned and wire fences cut.

My mother did something very bold, courageous, and insane. She actually caught a white man cutting one of the hog pen fences and at gunpoint, holding her .410 double-barrel shotgun on him, made him reconnect the wire in the fence (I shudder to think what could possibly have happened to her as a consequence of her actions).

After that incident, my parents received verbal and written threats. The rancher and doctor for whom my dad worked didn't take kindly to the threats. My siblings and I were told by my mother that a close friend of the doctor and rancher walked up and down the main street in Hayneville with a pistol in each hand, declaring what would happen if any one attempted to do him, the doctor, or my parents bodily harm.

Because of the threats, my parents decided to vacate the property as quickly as possible selling most of their livestock. With the help of relatives using horse-drawn wagons, they moved to my maternal grandmother's house, taking with them their household goods, chickens, a couple of horses and cows. At this juncture in their life, my parent's now had three children, my elder brother and my two older sisters. The younger of the two sisters was a toddler. My parents were married fourteen years before they successfully started a family.

My parents lived with my maternal grandmother until they could find a place of their own. They eventually found a place that they rented using some of the money from the sale of livestock and the property in Hayneville. This place was in no way as nice as the place they had previously bought. The doctor for whom my dad worked bought the property in Hayneville and later sold it.

Having left Hayneville, my father had to find another job. Luckily, the house my mom and dad rented was located near the dairy where my dad would eventually work. A friend of my father who worked at the dairy helped my father get a job there. Over the next five years, my younger sister and I were born. My mother continued to do some work picking cotton, but most of her time was spent at home with my siblings and me, tending livestock and fowl (guineas, turkeys, and chickens), working in her vegetable garden, and going fishing every chance she got.

From the union of my mother and father, there are six children (three boys and three girls). Our births occurred over a ten-year period. Interestingly, the girls were born on the seventeenth and the boys on the twenty-fifth. I would think this is quite unusual, and making this even more unusual is the birth of my middle sister and youngest sister on the seventeenth in the same month. My elder sister was born December 17; my middle and baby sisters were born July 17. My elder brother was born June 25, and my baby brother was born January 25. I was born September 25. This is probably quite unusual and a somewhat phenomenal occurrence. Below is a picture of each sibling shown in the order of birth first through sixth.

First   Second   Third

Fourth   Fifth   Sixth

A midwife delivered my three older siblings and me. My youngest sister and brother were born in a hospital in Montgomery, Alabama. All of my siblings and I have a light complexion. My elder sister and younger brother, however, have a skin tone that's slightly lighter. We all had black wavy hair when we were growing up.

My elder brother is five feet three inches tall and more visibly reflect our Asian heritage than the other siblings. My elder sister is five feet three inches and has facial features more reflective of the white heritage. She strongly resembles our paternal grandmother. My middle sister, baby sister, and I are five feet two, five feet four, and five feet eight inches tall, respectively, and have facial features that reflect a mixture of black, Native American, and white. My baby brother is the tallest of the siblings. He is six feet tall and has facial features that mostly reflect our white heritage.

As my siblings and I became teenagers, we had to take turns cooking, washing, and ironing. My mother told us that when we become adults, we need to be independent and shouldn't have to rely on anybody to cook, wash, or iron for us. My cooking didn't go very well. I cooked some biscuits once that were too hard for the dogs to eat. I didn't put enough shortening in them, and they were as hard as rocks. After that, I started paying my sisters a dollar or two dollars (whatever I could afford) to cook for me. Of the siblings, my elder brother, surprisingly, was the best cook. Cooking wasn't my forte. I did a much better job at washing and ironing. Today, I still wash and iron my clothes periodically, even though I am married. I guess old habits are hard to break.

All of my siblings and I generally got along well with each other. While each sibling, except for the two born in July, is under a different Zodiac sign and we each have a different personality, there are several qualities we have in common. One in particular is our strong work ethic when we were actively employed. This strong work ethic, I'm sure, is a replication of the work ethic demonstrated by our parents. My elder brother has always been focused, confident, dedicated to his work, outgoing, and goal oriented. My younger brother is also focused, confident, dedicated to his work, and outgoing. He is an avid hunter and fisherman. Like me, both my elder and younger brothers have a serious demeanor, curiosity and unwavering determination in achieving their goals.

My elder sister is the motherly, bossy type. She was also a dedicated worker, somewhat reserved, serious minded, and controlling. She also enjoys fishing. My middle sister is probably more low-key and less assertive than the other two sisters. She was a patient and methodical worker. She had a strong determination to do an excellent job. My youngest sister is the more vivacious, outgoing, and fun loving of the three. She also has always been goal oriented, loyal, and dedicated to accomplishing her work.

You will learn more about my personality and me as an individual as you continue to read this exposé. However, the one thing I will mention about myself now is that I have always had a spirit of giving—giving of my time and any money I had that I was in a position to share if someone in the family needed help. An example of my giving spirit is when I sacrificed spending money on myself and bought my younger brother a new car when he was in med school in Iowa. This was his first time living away from home in another state. The new car I bought him allowed him to have dependable transportation to come home when he got homesick and wanted to visit and spend time with family in Alabama. Having grown up extremely poor, I guess it was just my persona to be a caring and compassionate individual.

Housing And Living Conditions In Lowndes County

Lowndes County is situated in the south-central part of Alabama. It is one of several counties in the state that's located in what is referred to as the Black Belt Region (BBR). From an economic standpoint, the BBR is considered the poorest area in the state. Lowndes County is bounded on the north by Autauga County; on the east by Montgomery and Crenshaw Counties; on the south by Crenshaw, Butler, and Wilcox counties; and on the west by Wilcox and Dallas counties. The county is regular in outline except on the north, northeast, and northwest, where the boundary is formed by the Alabama River and its tributaries, Pintlalla Creek and Old Town Creek. The total area of the county is 708 square miles, or 453,120 acres. Lowndes County was created by an act in the general assembly approved January 20, 1830. The early settlers in Lowndes County came mainly from the states to the east and northeast. They grew cotton, corn, wheat, oats, hay and a variety of vegetables. Meat such as pork, beef, and mutton were produced at home as needed. Farms were practically self-sustaining.

When my parents were growing up in Lowndes County and when they were young adults, cotton was the leading crop and was grown on about 123,000 acres. Corn was the second crop of importance and was grown on approximately 36,000 acres. The average population of Lowndes County from 1950 to 1960 was 16,717. The largest town in the county had a population of less than 2,500, and the entire county was classified as rural. Lowndes County's population as of January 2016 is 11,299.

If you didn't live within the town limits of one of the small towns in the county, you usually lived in an area where your closest neighbor was an appreciable distance from you. It didn't matter if you were renting, buying, or if you owned your home, you needed to be where you could have a garden, raise chickens, a cow or two, pigs, or goats. You basically had to be self-supporting. If you didn't work at one of the small mills in Hayneville, there weren't any jobs of substance other than picking cotton. Because picking cotton was seasonal, it was not a steady source of income. In Lowndes County, where my family and I lived, there weren't any neighbors who lived in close proximity. We had more than adequate acreage to plant a large garden, raise livestock and fowl.

If you were black and poor and living in a rural area, it was difficult to find adequate housing. The house we lived in was much too small for a family of seven (parents and five children). It was old in appearance and not in good condition. It was wood framed with wooden floors. It had a tin roof, a front porch, rear steps, two bedrooms, one large open room which was a bedroom/living room combination and a small kitchen. The roof leaked, and the walls and floors had lots of cracks and holes. When it rained we used pots and pans to catch the water leaking inside the house from the roof. On a sunny day, you could see beams of sunlight shining through the cracks and holes. To plug up some of the holes and cracks, my parents saturated paper and burlap (feed bags) with a thick paste made of water and flour. The paste adhered to the wooden boards and would keep the paper and burlap from falling out of the holes and cracks.

During the winter months, the house was especially cold. It was almost as cold inside as outside. To keep us warm in bed at night, my mother made quilts. She made them using cotton, flour bags, cloth from old clothes, bed sheets and spreads. She wasn't concerned about the appearance of the quilts or their aesthetic value. She was only concerned about turning out a product that kept us warm. The cotton she used in making quilts was the cotton she picked that was left in the cotton fields, known as "scrapping." The cotton was relatively clean and was obviously used to give the quilts weight. The quilts weren't very attractive but we were more than glad to have them on our beds on cold, wintry nights.

There were no public utilities such as running water, electricity, or natural gas. Therefore, there was no indoor plumbing. We had an outhouse for a toilet. You can only imagine what it was like having to use the toilet in the cold of winter and the heat of summer. We used kerosene lamps, candles, flashlights, and kerosene lanterns for light. Water from a well and a spring near the house was water we used for drinking, cooking, bathing, washing dishes and clothes. In addition to using water from the well and spring, we collected rainwater in a five-gallon milk can, a two-gallon bucket, and a no. 4 tin tub. Rainwater was also used for washing clothes, and after it was boiled, it was used for washing fresh beef, meat from wild game, pork, fish, and fowl. Before rainwater was used, it was important not to disturb any debris that had settled at the bottom of the container. When it was finally used, it was carefully dipped or poured out of the container without disturbing the sediment.

During late spring and summer, it wasn't a good idea to collect rainwater in open containers left outside. Some species of mosquitoes in the Southern US lay their eggs on the walls of containers, and when rainwater fill the container, the eggs will hatch and the larvae will begin to develop. The mosquito in the aquatic stage is legless and wormlike (known as wrigglers). The larval stage is the time of growth and development for mosquitoes. Mosquito larvae grow rapidly. Under optimal conditions, some mosquitoes can complete their development (egg to pupa) in as little as four days. The pupa stage is generally rather short, lasting between one and three days. It ends when the adult mosquito emerges from the pupa skin at the surface of the water. At this point, the aquatic stages are over, and the aerial life of the mosquito begins. Mosquitoes usually mate in the air. Males will form a swarm in some conspicuous location and wait for females to fly into the swarm. When a female enters the swarm, she will be approached by males, which will then attempt to copulate with her. Mating is usually very brief and lasts for just a few seconds.

The only heat in the house we rented was from a fireplace in the living room. The fireplace was a good thing to have. In addition to using it to warm the house, it was used to fry and boil certain foods, heat water, make coffee, cook sweet potatoes and hoecakes (small cakes of bread made of cornmeal). Sweet potatoes and hoecakes were often cooked in the ashes underneath the fire in the fireplace. When they were done, they were placed on the concrete in front of the fireplace *or* in a tin pan to cool. Once the hoecakes were cool enough to eat, you simply picked one up, rubbed or blew the ashes off and ate it.

Most of the cooking (breakfast and dinner) was done on a wood-burning cast-iron stove. The stove was also used for making coffee, boiling water for drinking, bathing, washing dishes and clothes. Clothes were washed and rinsed in a no. 4 galvanized tin tub. When clothes were really dirty, they were placed in a ten-gallon washpot and boiled. The washpot was kept outside, and the water was heated using wood. A rubboard made of galvanized tin and wood was used to wash clothes. A no. 4 tin tub was used for bathing. Water for bathing when the weather was cold was heated in a kettle on the stove or in the fireplace or in the washpot. In spring and summer, water for bathing was often put in the tub and other containers and placed outside for the sun to heat.

Clothes were washed with Octagon soap or lye soap that my mother usually made. She purchased the lye at a combination grocery, hardware, and feed-and-seed store. To make the lye soap, she would place a certain amount of lye and tallow (beef fat) together in a hot cast-iron pot, stirring and cooking it until creamy. When it cooled and had become somewhat hard and solid, she cut it into squares and put it away in a small cardboard box in the coolest place she could find. Octagon soap was also used for bathing. After taking a bath with this highly alkaline soap, you didn't smell very good but you were clean.

After my family moved to Montgomery, my mother stopped making lye soap. She stopped making it because the tallow she needed was no longer readily available. She no longer had direct access to anyone who could get the tallow for her. However, she still had relatives in Lowndes County who continually made lye soap from whom she would occasionally get some. In the meantime, she continued to buy Octagon soap, which was sold in both grocery and drugstores. Therefore, we continued to use Octagon soap when clothes were washed and we took a bath. When our finances permitted, my mother would buy nicer smelling soap with which to bathe. She bought the cheapest soap she could buy that had a nice fragrance.

Galvanized Washtub   Cast-Iron Kettle

Wood-burning cast-iron stove   Washboard/Rubboard

Housing And Living Conditions In Rurban Montgomery

Montgomery is the capital of Alabama and is the county seat of Montgomery County. The city was founded and chartered in 1819 and was named for General Richard Montgomery, who was killed during the American Revolution. It became the political center for the state and was made the state capital in 1847. In 1861, during the American Civil War, it became the first capital of the Confederacy. It was captured by Union troops in 1865. After its recovery from the Civil War, Montgomery developed as an important center and market for cotton, livestock, yellow pine, and hardwood. Chief manufacturers in the city manufactured furniture and fertilizer. Maxwell and Gunter Air Force bases in the fifties and sixties added much to the civic, commercial, and cultural life of the city. Montgomery is the seat of Huntingdon College (1854) and Alabama State University (formerly Alabama State College). Alabama State College moved from Marion, Alabama, to Montgomery in 1887.

The population of Montgomery was about eight times the size of the population of the entire county of Lowndes. We moved to the outskirts of Montgomery on Christmas Day in 1950. We moved because the white man who owned the house and land where we lived told my parents he needed the land to raise cattle. This was a very inopportune time for us to move because my older siblings were in school and the move occurred in the middle of the school year. Thankfully, my father had already gotten a job driving for a prominent doctor who lived in Montgomery and also had his practice there. He got this job because the doctor he chauffeured when he lived in Hayneville recommended him. The two doctors were friends and often went quail hunting together. My father was happy because he enjoyed chauffeuring more than working at the dairy. Thank God, the doctor needed a chauffeur around the time we had to move.

The money from the sale of the livestock and property in Hayneville enabled my parents to be financially able to move to Montgomery. The money they received from the sale of livestock and property was only enough to buy three lots and make a down payment on a small house that was financed by the doctor for whom my father worked. The house in Montgomery was not much of an improvement over the one in Lowndes County. Similarly, it was also much too small for a family of seven, which became a family of eight when my baby brother was born. He was born about thirteen months after we moved.

The main difference in the house in Montgomery and the one in Lowndes County was the building materials used. The house in Montgomery was of cinder block with a concrete floor and a wooden roof that was covered with tar-paper shingles. The house consisted of a porch, rear steps, and four rooms—a living room, two bedrooms, and a kitchen. One bedroom was for my parents and the other one for my siblings and me. There were two full-size beds in the siblings' room. The girls slept in one bed and the boys in the other. We still didn't have indoor plumbing. The toilet was an outhouse and, because it had a concrete floor, was a step above the one in Lowndes County. The concrete floor was very important because during the winter months, you could burn wood or paper in a metal bucket or directly on the floor to keep warm.

Shortly after moving into the cinder-block house, we decided we needed to paint it but didn't have the money to buy the paint we needed. Since the house was cinder block, we decided the cheapest, easiest, and quickest thing we could do was whitewash it. Whitewash is a mixture of lime and water. The whitewash worked well on the cinder block because the cinder block is very porous and absorbent. Lime was relatively cheap, and the brush specially made for white-washing cinder block was affordable.

Although the neighborhood to which we moved in Montgomery was in the city limits, it didn't have public utilities. Therefore, we were faced with the same heating, cooking, washing, and water issues we were faced with when we lived in Lowndes County. A different problem, however, with which we were faced was flooding. The neighborhood was in a low-lying area. Therefore, when the Montgomery area got an excessive amount of rain the neighborhood flooded.

When we moved to Montgomery, there was little improvement in living conditions. My parents moved to the neighborhood because this was what they could afford and they knew several families living there that previously lived in Lowndes County. It seemed that city government had forgotten the neighborhood existed. Was it because the neighborhood was all black? Was money an issue? Whatever the reason, it seemed there was nobody in city government interested in improving the city's overall infrastructure.

Since there were no public utilities in the neighborhood, a wood- or coal-burning cast-iron heater was placed in the living room and each bedroom to provide heat. Even though we were in a house devoid of cracks and holes, staying warm in autumn and winter continued to be a concern. Fortunately, my mother stayed the course in her quilt making for a while and even sold a few to neighbors. For cooking, we continued to use a wood-burning stove. A cast iron pump for extracting water from the ground was used to get water for drinking, cooking, washing dishes, washing clothes, and bathing. To get water via the hand pump, a hole about two and one-half inches wide was drilled deep into the ground until an underground water stream was reached. When the driller determined how much pipe was needed, a two-inch cast-iron pipe with a filter attached was placed in the hole, reaching the underground water stream. The hand pump was connected to the pipe and mounted on a wooden platform to hold it in place. Before water could be pumped using the hand pump, the pump had to be primed (pipe filled with water reaching the underground stream). Water for priming the pump was kept outside or inside in a closed container. A no. 4 tub as usual was used for washing and rinsing clothes and for bathing.

Wood or coal burning
cast-iron heater

Cast-iron pump

Since our move to Montgomery was somewhat abrupt and unexpected, and my three older siblings were attending school in Lowndes County, school was an issue my parents were not in a position to address. The move from the Lowndes County school system to the Montgomery system, and the timeframe in which this move occurred, had an adverse impact on my older siblings in terms of their grade level placement. It appears that my parents and older siblings having had to move several times when they lived in Lowndes County, and our moving to Montgomery in the middle of the school year, caused my elder brother and sister to lose one grade level in Lowndes County and one in Montgomery. My second sister lost one grade level as a result of the move to Montgomery. I'm not sure what effect, if any, this may have had on them psychologically. Maybe they were too young to be aware of what happened or they were too preoccupied with the move to Montgomery to think about anything else.

Nonetheless, they each lost at least one grade level, and I never heard them discuss it. Apparently, losing one or two grade levels was never an issue for them. I believe my siblings and I were just happy to be in a place where we were surrounded by neighbors and children our age with whom we could interact and play. It was nice to be someplace where we didn't feel so isolated and didn't have to chase pigs, chickens and climb trees to have fun. It was refreshing to have kids other than siblings with whom to play.

Although we were living in a different environment, one thing remained constant—we were still poor. This reminds me of the adage, "The more things change, the more they remain the same." In the mid '50s, the doctor for whom my dad worked died and left him enough money to add two rooms (a bedroom for the girls and a new kitchen) to our house. There was a small loan balance on the original house that was forgiven. The old kitchen was converted to a dining room. A den and bathroom were eventually added when we got sewer lines and running water in the neighborhood and the city made low-interest rate loans available for upgrading homes. Before our house was upgraded and modernized, we had an eight-by-eight-foot wooden storage house in the backyard that was used for washing clothes, housing small tools, lawn equipment, the lawn mower and a variety of miscellaneous items. We also had a fenced-in chicken yard with chicken coops and a small crib that was used for storing carpentry and gardening tools, chicken feed, short (a by-product of wheat milling that consist of bran, germ, and coarse meal) for dog food, fertilizer, and surplus building materials.

To keep stray animals out of our yard, my dad installed a fence across the front part of the property. Our neighbors living on the side and rear of us had already installed fences on their adjoining property. Because we couldn't afford a chain-link fence, a cheap medium-gauge wire fence, configured in four-by-four-inch squares, that was three feet wide and several feet long was erected. Two sheets of fencing were vertically and horizontally connected to make the fence six foot high. For privacy and also to delineate property lines, hedges were planted along the fence. To beautify the yard, evergreen shrubs and a variety of flowers and flowering trees (hydrangea, dogwood, magnolia, redbud, and holly) that grew wild in Butler County were transplanted in our yard. Several fruit trees (two peach, two apple, three plum, and a fig) were also planted. Additionally, two pecan trees and a grape vine were planted. Runners from St. Augustine grass my father got from the grass in the doctor's yard were planted in our yard, which eventually grew into a beautiful lawn.

In autumn and winter, we took a bath on the weekend and "washed up" during the week. A tin foot tub (about one-eighth the size of a no. 4 tin tub) was used to soak and wash our feet and a wash pan (porcelain basin) was used to wash other body parts. The weekend, especially during the nine months school was in session, was the only time you could find the time and privacy to take a bath. Preparing to take a bath was quite time consuming. First, you had to heat enough water on the cast-iron heater, which took a while; second, you had to make several trips outside to pump the water and bring it inside using the foot tub or a two-gallon tin bucket. To keep warm while you bathed, the tub had to be placed relatively close to the cast-iron heater. Therefore, there was always the danger of getting too close to the heater and making contact. On one occasion, I did exactly that—I got too close. I inadvertently dropped the soap in the tub, and when I bent over to pick it up, not realizing how close I had gotten to the heater, I immediately felt pain and heard something sizzle. Today I still have a scar on my right buttock to remind me of the close encounter I had with the heater that day. My middle and youngest sisters also had close encounters with the same heater.

Every time I went swimming in the creek on the farm in Butler County, I considered that as my bath for the day. The place I swam in the creek had a sandy bottom and the water was crystal clear. Amazingly, much of the creek bed and bank were limestone and sand. Along the creek bank as the creek meandered through the property were beautiful magnolia trees, ferns, and wild hydrangea. I went swimming every chance I got.

My parents usually took a bath on the weekend. However, my mother, I am sure, would sometimes take a bath when my siblings and I were at school. During the summer, when school was out, she would sometimes take a bath while my siblings and I were outside playing. When it came to bathing during the spring and summer months, my father had an excellent idea. On hot and humid days, when he was at work and was hot and sweaty from working outside, he would connect a hose to the tank in the pump house and take a bath. I always wondered why my father kept a change of underwear, socks, and a ragged towel in the Jeep.

The pump house was slightly elevated with a concrete and gravel floor designed for water to drain. Yep! I took a bath in the pump house a few times myself. The soap we used was a bar of bath soap my father "borrowed" from the boss lady's bathroom. Taking a bath in the pump house was a lot quicker, easier, and more private than taking a bath at home. When I finished bathing in the pump house, I would wash and wring the water out of my underwear (cotton briefs) and use them as if they were a towel. When I finished, I rinsed them in clear water and took them home to dry. When my dad and I could, we took a bath and hosed down with water that was stored in the tank because it was a lot warmer than the water we would get from the tank if the pump was running and water was being pumped directly from the ground.

Growing Up In Lowndes County And Rurban Montgomery

I'm the fourth of six siblings. I was born in Burkville, Alabama in 1946. Burkville is located in rural Northeast Lowndes County. When I lived in Lowndes County, I was quite young. However, there are several things I experienced that I vividly remember. I remember the house in which we lived, the garden, fowl (chickens, guineas, and turkeys), pigs, three cows and two horses. I also remember the crib and the front yard that had a huge oak tree in the center of it. There was no grass in the yard, and my mother always kept the yard free of leaves and debris. She used branches from a plum tree to clean the yard of debris. The branches of the plum tree had stickers on them that would pull leaves and small sticks like a rake. To get the yard really clean, she swept it with a straw broom. The straw broom was also used to sweep and clean the floor inside the house.

I lived in Lowndes County four years and three months. While living there, three memorable things happened with which I was either directly or indirectly involved that I would like to share with you. The three things that occurred are as follows:

(1) While I was outside playing one autumn afternoon, my father and a neighbor slaughtered a yearling calf. I observed them dress out the calf. When they gutted the

calf, everything in the rib cage and abdominal cavity were discarded except the heart, kidneys, tripe and liver. To my amazement, they took the liver of the calf and cooked it in the ashes underneath the fire they had in the yard. When the liver was done, my dad gave me a slice of it to eat. It was tender and delicious. I ate another slice. As I ate it, I thought to myself, *This is some good liver.* A meal or something to eat was always welcomed, and maybe this was why the liver tasted so good. The ashes on the liver were very light and fine and were easily rubbed or blown off. Therefore, there was no reason for my dad or me to be concerned about me ingesting any of the ashes. However, being as young as I was, I'm sure I didn't thoroughly remove all of the ashes and, as a result, ingested a few.

(2) My mother took me with her one morning when she went outside to milk the Jersey milk cow we owned. She carried with her a two gallon tin bucket and a stool to sit on. In the bucket, she had some water and a cloth that she used to wash the mammary glands (tits) of the cow before she started milking. After washing the tits, she poured the water out of the bucket, dried it out with the cloth, and proceeded to milk the cow. Milking a cow requires some skill and finesse. I say this because she let me try milking the cow and when I grabbed a tit with several fingers wrapped around it and pulled down on it, no milk came out. When I observed my mother milk the cow, I noticed she first placed her thumb downward toward the palm of her hand and then placed it against one of the tits. Second, she wrapped her forefinger (index finger) and the finger next to it around the same tit. Third, she gently squeezed the tit while pulling it down using a downward thrusting motion. Out came the milk. This technique was repeated until she got the desired amount of milk. Since the cow's udder (milk bag) has several mammary glands, both hands can be used during the milking process. Milking isn't as

easy as it sounds. Believe me, you need some practice before you can perfect the technique.

(3) My father didn't just raise two or three cows; he also raised a few hogs. One summer afternoon, while I was outside playing, I decided to catch one of the piglets wandering around in the yard. When I attempted to catch the piglet, it ran underneath the floor of the crib. I was determined to catch the piglet. So I decided to crawl underneath the crib's floor behind it. I quickly discovered the piglet had escaped on the other side. I couldn't go forward or backward. There was very little space between the ground and the floor of the crib. I couldn't raise my arms and knees high enough to slide backward. I could only go forward, and I was nowhere near a side of the crib where I could crawl or slide out. I was very frightened. My heart was racing, and I could hardly breathe. I yelled for help. Finally, after what seemed like an eternity, my father came to my rescue. He removed two boards, and I was able to climb out. As I climbed out, my dad could see I was frightened. To help me calm down, he fluffed my hair and gently patted me on my back with his right hand. In a calm voice, he cautioned me not to chase a piglet under the crib again. He wasn't upset with me because he knew I didn't have any toys to play with and I was just doing something to have fun. Needless to say, after such a frightening ordeal, I never had a desire to chase another piglet.

The neighborhood to which we moved in Montgomery was rurban (several neighbors did some small-scale farming, raised hogs, chickens, and planted gardens). It was relatively small and located on the outskirts of the city southwest of the downtown area. The neighborhood didn't have any of the amenities of the inner city, such as a park, streetlights, traffic lights, stop signs, paved streets, or sidewalks. There were seven streets in the neighborhood allowing traffic to flow north and south. At the north end of each street was a wide ditch and a set of elevated railroad tracks about five feet high. You could cross the tracks only when the water in the ditch was low or the ditch was dry.

Each street was about two tenths of a mile long. These streets were evenly divided through the middle by an avenue (approximately four-tenths of a mile long) that allowed traffic to flow east and west. Each street was parallel to the other and the same length except Fourth Street and Seventh Street. Fourth Street and Seventh Street were half the length of the others. They were shorter because there were several businesses, including a hardware store, a grocery store, a construction business, and some vacant land, situated where the first half of the streets would have been placed.

I lived on Second Street. The surface of this street and the other streets also was a mixture of clay and gravel. Houses in the neighborhood were a mixture of wood frame and cinder block except for maybe three small brick houses. These houses were owned by three of the more affluent neighbors. One of the neighbors cleaned bricks for a living for home and commercial builders, another owned a beauty shop and was a very successful beautician, and the third one was a private duty Licensed Practical Nurse.

Located in the neighborhood, at the north end of Third Street, was a combination junk-food store and nightclub named Chicken Shack Inn. The club was not an attractive structure. It was in need of some carpentry work and a fresh coat of paint. During the day, the owner sold a sundry of items such as cigarettes, beer, sodas, chips, ice cream, cookies, and candy. At night, it was a popular night club that provided jukebox music. Occasionally, there was live entertainment on the weekends. The club, consisting of several small adjunct rooms, was somewhat secluded and had a large patio out back with tables and lots of trees. The patio was near a small fenced-in pond where the owner kept his pet alligator named Baby.

The club was widely known among blacks in the Montgomery area for the partying that took place there mostly on the weekends. It was so well known that the neighborhood was nicknamed Chicken Shack. When I became a teenager, I realized that the neighborhood was nicknamed Chicken Shack because of the way the neighborhood evolved and because of the shabby structural appearance of houses and the club. Hence, the shabby houses and the club's name were seen as an actual reflection and description of housing in the neighborhood. If I told someone where I lived, the individual would immediately and emphatically say Chicken Shack that, in most instances, had an intentionally demeaning connotation.

Unfortunately, we didn't have a playground in the neighborhood. We played kickball, touch football, and stickball in the streets. A tennis ball was used in place of a real baseball, and a broom or mop handle was used for the bat. For several years, the folk for whom my dad worked lived adjacent to the governor's mansion, which had a tennis court. Occasionally, he would find tennis balls in his employer's yard that had been knocked over the wall and fence separating the two properties. He would bring the balls home and give them to me. These were the tennis balls we used when we played stickball. Most of the time, I played stickball, kickball, and football barefooted in the street and, as a result, cut and bruised my feet countless times on the sharp rocks in the gravel.

We used a vacant lot to play basketball. The basketball goal was made using the tire rim of a small bicycle tire and scrap wooden boards. A few kids who owned roller skates skated in the streets even though the street's surface wasn't a good surface for skating. Periodically, the kids would skate on the highway (the highway had an asphalt surface) near the neighborhood when the traffic wasn't heavy.

Store-bought toys were few and far between. Most of the kids in the neighborhood didn't have nice store-bought toys. When I was age ten, my parents bought me a cowboy outfit and cap pistols for Christmas. Only a few kids owned a bicycle. Owning a bicycle was exciting. I didn't get a bicycle until I was age fourteen. I got it for Christmas, and I was really excited although I helped pay for it. I don't think I went to sleep Christmas Eve night. The next day, it seemed like I rode nonstop until I had an unpleasant experience with three Gypsies who pulled knives on me and took my bike. A family of Gypsies lived off the main highway in the neighborhood between Second and Third Streets. The mother in the family was a fortune teller. One of the Gypsies actually held a knife on my throat. I was defenseless and more angry than afraid because I couldn't defend myself. They didn't take the bike to steal it; they just wanted to go joyriding. However, pulling their knives on me to take my bike that I hardly had an opportunity to ride didn't sit well with me. All I could think about was they intended to do me bodily harm if I didn't give them the bicycle. I was angry. I knew where my daddy kept his pistol and shotgun, but I used my better judgment and didn't get either of the weapons.

An older cousin, some friends, and I armed with real baseball bats got my bike back. It appeared this was the right thing to do. After all, the Gypsies had knives, and we felt we needed something to defend ourselves. They got the message loud and clear that my bike was off-limits. I never had an encounter with them after that and noticed a short while later they had moved out of the neighborhood.

From the incident with the Gypsies, I learned a valuable lesson at a young age that has helped me in life. After I calmed down and thought about what could have happened, I realized the importance of thinking before you act and to always think about the consequences of your actions. This is a good rule of thumb in most situations especially volatile situations. Unfortunately, the cousin who helped me retrieve my bike from the gypsies lost his life to an act of violence involving craps because he didn't follow this rule. He and one of our neighbors were involved in an altercation over a quarter, and my cousin was stabbed in the heart. Certain types of knives, guns, and ammo should be kept in a secure place preferably under lock and key. We certainly don't want someone (especially a minor), due to our carelessness, do something brutal to somebody or commit an act of violence that one will regret the rest of his/her life. The bike was something material and could have been replaced. I continued to enjoy riding my bike until I got my driver's license and gave the bike to my younger brother.

In today's society, especially in several major cities in the US, there are too many guns on the streets and too much violence involving young blacks where guns are used as a deadly force. Life is the most valuable and precious gift there is. We have only one life, and once it's gone, it cannot be replaced. Something has to continue to be done to take guns off the streets and out of the hands of young black males. Parents have to get more involved. I feel that parents or guardians of youngsters under age twenty-one who are in the house-hold should be held accountable. Parents need to be aware of their children's activities and become more knowledgeable of their where-abouts. It is imperative that parents take time to talk with their chil-dren and do a better job of communicating with them.

Young mothers (many of whom are teenagers and don't have the emotional maturity and necessary parenting skills) should seek guidance from relatives, neighbors, ministers, educators, and other professionals in raising their children. Black fathers, whether they are in the same household or not, must get more involved in their sons' and daughters' lives and be a positive influence in helping them grow emotionally, psychologically, and intellectually. Even though Big Brothers Big Sisters organizations continue to play a major role in serving as good role models mostly for single parent children, the parents need to ensure that they are doing everything they can do to likewise be good role models. While children need all the love, nur-turing, and moral support that they can get from their parents, they also need their parents to fulfill their commitment to put forth the effort needed to instill in them the right values.

In addition to encouraging more parental involvement in mon-itoring activities of adolescents and young adults, the police depart-ment and city government officials in cities where there is a serious gun-control problem might want to implement a long-term curfew and consider the establishment of a police gun-control unit (PGCU). The unit would be equipped with body cameras and long-range metal detection devices and would devote all of its time, 24/7, exclusively to gun control. To minimize possible complaints of harassment, etc., the establishment of the PGCU would be widely publicized and each member of the PGCU would wear a body camera. The unit would have the authority to search anyone suspected of carrying a firearm and arrest anyone with an illegal firearm in his/her possession. If a firearm is found in the possession of a minor, the parent(s) or person having custody would be counseled by a designated member of the PGCU regarding gun control, gun safety, and parental accountability with emphasis on parental vigilance and accountability. In the interim, those individuals illegally carrying firearms could be psychologically evaluated by qualified law-enforcement personnel to try and determine why the perpetrators are drawn to violence.

Domestic violence is on the rise. Are these acts of violence and others the results of a lack of spirituality, self-hatred, anger, and hostility evolving out of social and/or economic despair and frustration? Is the violence among blacks and in black families caused by systemic indoctrination stemming from slavery that it is okay to brutalize each other or take a black person's life because it has little value? Maybe psychological evaluations of perpetrators in domestic violence by law-enforcement personnel could also be used to determine why there is so much domestic violence and develop a strategy and plan of action to curb it. We have to continue to look for answers. The gun buyback program helped take some guns out of circulation but we still have too many on the streets and in the home that are used to commit violent and senseless crimes.

It's time to be more creative and to try different approaches in attempts to reduce and hopefully eliminate criminal and domestic acts of violence especially where guns are used. One approach is for city government to solicit suggestions and recommendations directly from the public including teenagers and young adults. I believe teenagers and young adults (twenty-one to thirty-five years of age) are in a position to provide invaluable input. They hear, know, and see things that older adults are not aware of. They would have a different perspective of why some of their peers are violent or become violent. In many instances where the gun is used in acts of violence, it appears the perpetrator acted without thinking about the consequences of his actions and the negative effects they would have on the victim's family and his family as well. Both families are adversely affected emotionally, psychologically, and financially. The same as the gun problem, we have to continue to look for answers as to why black-on-black crimes occur at a high rate and hopefully find a solution to this disturbing problem as well.

Prior to adolescence, most of my toys I owned were homemade or simply, just a piece of wood or a stick I would find and pretend it was a pony, guitar, microphone, shotgun, pistol, knife, or sword. Using my sticks, I played a lot of cowboys and Indians, pretended I was a soldier, and did a lot of make-believe small-game hunting.

All of my kites were homemade. I used newspaper that my dad brought home from work, dog fennel weed (a strong-scented weed of the chamomile of Europe and Asia naturalized along roadsides in the US), flour paste, kite cord, and strips of clothing from old clothes for the kite's tail. The kite's frame was made from the dog fennel weed. This weed, when it dries, is very light, somewhat flexible, and relatively strong. The inside of the weed resembles a foam substance in appearance and texture. If you cut or break the weed, you will find the weed is narrowly hollow. Flying my homemade kites was fun. Some of my friends and I occasionally competed with each other to see who could make the fancier kite and who could fly his kite the highest and farthest.

My bow and arrows were also homemade. I used a flexible green limb from a hardwood tree and white packing cord or a single string of twine to make the bow. A dog fennel weed was used for the arrow. The dog fennel weed grew in abundance, and because of its' availability, it was the best thing I could find and use to make an arrow. The weed from the bottom up is somewhat broad, and then it narrows. Usually, a top from a soda pop was attached at the tip of the narrow end of the weed o give it weight and balance. A slit was put in the big end of the weed and taped or wrapped with kite cord to keep it from splitting. A small section of the soda pop top was flattened, and with a pair of pliers, the flattened part of the top was squeezed around the tip of the weed, applying just enough pressure to tighten it without breaking the weed. If I didn't have access to a pair of pliers, I used a large rock or a brick.

Popular store-bought toys for boys were the yo-yo, spinning top, and marbles. This spinning top was the old-fashioned pear-shaped one that was spun with a string. Most boys usually bought marbles and the game of marbles was very popular. Marble games were very competitive and usually had two, three, or four players. To start the game, a large circle was drawn and each player placed an equal number of marbles inside the circle. We always played "keepers." This means that when the game was over, you kept the marbles you had in your possession that you knocked out of the circle. To decide who would shoot first, a horizontal line was drawn about ten feet above the circle. The player that placed his marble (referred to as his "toy") closest to the circle without going inside would shoot first. The next closest would shoot second and so on. To start the competition, each player would return to the line and shoot but this time trying to place his toy inside the circle. The first shooter starts the competition by using his toy to knock as many marbles out of the circle as possible until he either missed or failed to knock one out. Each player would continue to take turns shooting until there were no marbles left in the circle.

In marbles, you could knock your opponent's toy out of the circle when it was your turn to shoot but if you missed, you lost your turn. On the other hand, if you hit your target, your opponent would have to shoot from the spot where his toy stopped. Another facet of marbles was "partners" (four players with two on each team). Partners allowed you and your partner to take turns shooting when it was either his or your turn to shoot. This was interesting because if a lot of the marbles were in close proximity to your partner's toy, he could shoot instead of you and vice versa. This gave your team the advantage and usually allowed your team to dominate the game.

I loved the game of marbles. So much so I wore holes in the knees of my pants. If you really wanted to get a good aim at the marble you were attempting to knock out of the circle, you almost always had to get on your knees. After doing this over and over, you wore holes in the knees of your pants. Often, there were times when it was to your advantage to shoot from a standing position. Shooting from a standing position required a lot of skill. However, if you were as good as I was (not bragging), you could shoot from a standing position and hit your target consistently. I rarely missed my target. When I stopped playing marbles, I had accumulated several gallons of marbles of all colors and various sizes that I gave to my baby brother and other boys in the neighborhood.

Games and activities that girls and boys enjoyed playing together were hopscotch, jacks, jump rope, paddleball, dodge-ball, and hula-hoop. Hula-hoop and jump rope were the most popular among girls. Hopscotch and jacks seemed to be equally enjoyed by both girls and boys.

Hopscotch was a game played in which a player tossed an object, usually a flat stone or other flat object, into areas of a figure outlined on the ground and then hopped through the figure and back using one or both feet as the figure required in order to retrieve the stone. As a player, your goal was to successfully place the stone in the box outlined on the ground in order of progression and then retrieve it without making a mistake. If you, the player, misplaced your foot or feet you lost your turn and the next player would start.

Jacks were played using thirteen small six-pointed metal objects and a small rubber ball. The object of the game is to bounce the ball, pick up the jack(s) while the ball is in the air, and catch it in the same hand. The player would continue picking up jacks each time increasing the number until all thirteen are picked up at once while catching the ball. If at any time the player does not successfully pick up the jacks while catching the ball, you lost your turn. Often it was a lot of fun just spinning jacks to see how long you could make one or several spin simultaneously. Other games that both boys and girls played together were hide-and-seek, doctor-and-nurse, and Simon says. The most popular of the three was Simon says with hide-and-seek, doctor-and-nurse second and third, respectively.

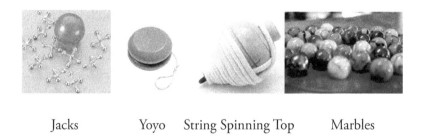

Jacks   Yoyo   String Spinning Top   Marbles

Everybody in the neighborhood knew each other and generally got along well with one another. However, when my family moved to the neighborhood, we would often hear comments from other kids like "they think they are white" or "they think they are better than us." In my opinion, we did nothing to warrant these remarks. We couldn't quite understand the hostility because several families already living in the neighborhood consisted of light-skinned adults and children. The remarks were annoying, but we managed not to overreact. Overreacting could have very easily resulted in fisticuffs or some other act of physical violence.

The only potentially combatant situation involved my middle sister and a girl who lived down the street from us. There was some bullying that took place because most of the boys my sister's age and the bully's age found my sister attractive and the young lady was apparently jealous of the attention my sister was getting. My sister was petite and half the size of the bully. When my sister and I were getting ready for school one morning, I noticed she had an extremely long hatpin in her hand. I asked her what she was planning to do with it. She told me if the bully attacked her, she was going to scratch the bully's eyes out with it. In the meantime, the bully attacked the twin sisters of a slightly older girl who lived up the street from the bully. In retaliation, the older sister went to the house of the bully, called her out, and proceeded to beat her bloody. Consequently, the bully's bullying in the neighborhood stopped. Please note that I am in no way suggesting that a violent act of this nature is the solution. I'm merely stating what happened.

Bullying is nothing new. It has been around for a long time. Bullying today, however, is much more violent sometimes resulting in serious injury or death of the person bullied. Bullying, in most cases, has a devastating effect on the victim emotionally and psychologically. I strongly believe that school officials should use a direct approach in dealing with bullying with a zero tolerance. In school assembly meetings, bullying should be openly discussed and addressed with emphasis on the detrimental effects of it. School administrators should ensure that qualified school personnel such as girls' and boys' counselors are properly trained and equipped to deal with situations involving bullying. Counselors and other appropriate school personnel, and parents as well, should be proactive in dealing directly with bullying and situations involving bullying.

My family was the only family in the neighborhood that all the children were very light skinned. Maybe our light skin color reminded some of the neighbors of the social inequality, disparity, and injustice that existed between blacks and whites. It was almost like we were ostracized. It wasn't blatant but just enough to be noticed. After we lived in the neighborhood for a short while and the neighbors could see that we were poor and just trying to survive like everybody else, their attitude changed, and we were better accepted. Eventually, nobody ever mentioned skin color, and several families on our street became our close friends and we treated each other like blood relatives.

We lived over two miles from the nearest public school. Therefore, we rode the school bus to and from school. If you were transported via school bus, you were usually called country, looked down on, and sometimes the object of derogatory gestures and comments. When I got my bicycle, I would ride it to school when I had band practice after school or had to go to work. Riding the school bus wasn't much fun. During the winter months, you almost froze to death, and in late spring, you were lucky if you didn't suffer from heat exhaustion. On the other hand, though, riding the school bus did have a couple of advantages: you didn't have to walk to school when it was freezing cold outside or storming and raining.

As soon as I got home from school each day, I ate dinner, and then I had to do my after-school chores. The first thing I always did was chop firewood and kindling for the stove. During the winter months, I also had to chop enough fire wood and kindling for the heaters. After school and on the weekends, my older brother worked part time as a waiter at a restaurant. Therefore, I was responsible for doing most of the laborious chores. He worked full time during the summer. The restaurant was for whites only and was about two miles from where we lived. When I became age sixteen, I thought about applying for a job at the restaurant but never did because my father told me he needed me to work with him to pick up the slack when he was running errands or out of the city. If I had gotten a job at the restaurant, I'm sure I would have made more money. Since my sisters couldn't chop firewood and carry heavy buckets of coal, I guess I was at the age that chores and tasks around the house requiring physical strength were my responsibility. Other chores I was expected to do included mowing grass, trimming shrubbery and hedges, raking leaves, and tilling soil (I used a fork and shovel) for the vegetable gardens. We did not own a tiller.

When I finished my chores, I had to do my homework. It was usually late in the evening when I finished, and quite often I was physically tired and found it hard to concentrate. I would sometimes fall asleep. To be able to see how to read and do my homework, I had to use a kerosene lamp or a candle for light. The main source of light at night was a kerosene lamp in each room.

In the early '60s, electricity was the first public utility we got. Hence, we little by little were able to get electric ceiling lights, lamps, a fan, and an electric heater. We eventually got a party-line phone and an electric toaster. When we got natural gas, running water, and sewer lines, which was also in the early '60s, we eventually bought a gas stove and a gas heater. When finances permitted, we had a kitchen sink installed, added a bathroom complete with a bathtub, sink, and commode.

There were seven boys close to my age who lived on the street on which I lived. We all became friends. We played sports and other games together in the neighborhood and rode the school bus together. The family of one of the boys who lived several houses down the street from me was the first to get a black-and-white television. The father worked at a motel not far from the neighborhood, and I surmise he may have bought a TV through the motel at a discount or purchased one of the old TVs when they were replaced with new ones. We were all excited. Almost every afternoon for a while, several of us would gather on the floor in the living room at the friend's house and watch *The Secret Storm*, *The Edge of Night*, and *The Lone Ranger*. On Saturday morning, we would occasionally visit to watch cartoons. My favorite cartoon was the *Smurfs*.

Eventually, my family got a black-and-white television, and everyone in the family was thrilled. Only three of the seven boys who lived on my street graduated high school, and I'm the only one who attended college. All of us, when we became adults, got married and started a family. Three of the guys still live in Montgomery. Interestingly, the one who was the first one on our street to get a TV still lives in the family home that he inherited. Three of the guys live in Detroit, Michigan, and one lives in Gary, Indiana. Two of the three who live in Detroit got jobs in the automobile industry and the one in Gary got a job in the steel industry. One of the guys in Detroit I haven't seen in about fifty-two years, and I don't know if he is still alive.

Most of the guys and some of the girls who lived in the neighborhood my age and older dropped out of school and got minimum-wage jobs working at motels, hotels, hospitals, service stations, fast-food establishments, the airport, the stockyard, and various other businesses in the city. A few of the guys worked as carpenters and mechanics. One of the guys owned and operated a barber shop at his house for a while. He was a self-taught barber and never got a license to legally operate a barber shop. He was a good friend and would occasionally cut my hair. I paid fifty cents for a haircut.

Fortunately, some of the guys and girls from the neighborhood eventually got good paying jobs and were financially able to send their kids to college. Several of the kids earned advanced degrees and worked in various professions such as law, politics, education, medicine, business, and accounting. The barber had several younger sisters who graduated college and earned advanced degrees. Phenomenally, one of the fellows in the neighborhood several years my junior, currently owns and operates a successful grocery store chain in and outside the Montgomery area. He is also involved in several other businesses. Also, one of my cousins from the neighborhood currently owns and operates a very successful restaurant. Another one of the guys is currently a general contractor. Several older guys who lived in the neighborhood were drafted in the army, and one enlisted in the navy. Two of the guys drafted in the army served twenty years. The one who enlisted in the navy served twenty-five years.

Interestingly, many of the kids who grew up in the neighborhood still live in their parents', grandparents', or great grandparents' homes. Homes today have been remodeled and are much more comfortable and attractive. Presently, there are several new and relatively new brick homes throughout the neighborhood. The old church in the neighborhood has been replaced with a modern brick church, with a large concrete and asphalt parking lot. The church membership has grown significantly. A lot of the members live throughout the Montgomery area.

A few of us from the neighborhood periodically talked about having a neighborhood reunion. On September 26, 2015, we had our first reunion. The reunion was planned on short notice. Therefore, a lot of former residents presently residing out of town didn't have an opportunity to attend. Locals, however, showed up in a big way. Over four hundred reunion T-shirts were sold. Since a lot of folks take some vacation days Labor Day weekend, we decided to make the reunion an annual Labor Day weekend event.

Religious Denomination

I grew up in the Christian Methodist Episcopal Church (CME). My family and I were members of the first CME church of Lowndesboro, Alabama. The church was built in the early 1830s. The church still stands today. It is a gabled structure with a portico across the entire front supported by four wooden columns. Inside, narrow stairs wind on either side to the balcony across the rear of the church. On the roof is a small octagonal gable topped with the copper-plated dome that once graced the state capitol at Cahaba. The Methodist-Protestant church acquired the dome from the original state capitol after a flood in 1833 that caused the original capitol to collapse. Major William Robinson, wishing to retain a relic of the Cahaba capitol, brought the dome to Lowndesboro. There was a dispute among the members, and all except two families left the church. After the death of Major Robinson in the 1880s, the building and property was deeded to a group of former slaves and their children. Services continued in the church until 1966. The building was abandoned in 1983. In 1990, it was leased by a local taskforce for fifty years. It has been restored by the Lowndesboro Historical Society and designated as a historical monument.

I joined church at age nine. At age twelve, I started teaching Sunday school and, for several years, taught kids in my age group and younger. I was asked by the pastor to teach because I was a good reader and I did a good job with biblical terminology. Generally, the adults in the church weren't well educated. The class I taught was held in the choir stand away from the adult class. Only the teachers had

Sunday school books so the Bible was used exclusively by members in the Sunday school classes. The pastor gave me a printed outline for the lesson, which included a few talking points and scripture to read and discuss. Teaching Sunday school basically involved facilitating the reading of scripture and interactive interpretation of scripture. If there was something I didn't understand or had questions about, this was discussed with the pastor. When everybody reassembled in the sanctuary after Sunday school, the superintendent of the Sunday school did the summary and closeout.

The church in Lowndesboro is approximately twenty miles from where we lived and is located northwest of Montgomery. Because the church was in a rural area with a small membership, Sunday school and church services were held only twice a month on the first and third Sunday. On second and fourth Sundays, my family and I usually attended the neighborhood Baptist church located across the street from our house. It didn't matter that this church was Baptist because we were only interested in hearing the sermon. Church doctrine didn't come into play. Occasionally, we attended a small CME church located down the street from the elementary school I attended. Biweekly church service and Sunday school were common for small rural CME churches. Revival at the church was always held during a week leading into the first or third Sunday.

There was a small cemetery down the street from the church where most of the church members and their relatives were buried. To my knowledge, the cemetery was an old cemetery for blacks who existed during slavery. Family members were responsible for planting flowers, shrubs and keeping gravesites clean. My father was initially buried, there but my elder sister, with the other siblings' concurrence, had his burial vault exhumed and transferred to a cemetery in Montgomery where my mother is also buried.

The CME church was organized in 1870 when several black ministers, with the support of their white counterparts in the former Methodist Episcopal Church, South, met to form an organization that would allow them to establish and maintain their own political organization. This allowed them to ordain their own bishops and ministers without the necessity of their being officially endorsed or appointed by the white-dominated body. They called this fellowship the Colored Methodist Episcopal Church, which it remained until their successors adopted the current name in the 1950s. In the CME church, bishops are administrative superintendents of the church. They are elected by "delegate" votes for as many years deemed until the age of seventy-four, when he/she must retire. Their duties include appointing clergy to serve local churches as pastor, performing ordinations, and safeguarding the doctrine and discipline of the church. CME bishops may be male or female and serve for four-year terms. The bishops represent the executive branch of the government structure. The general council represents the legislative branch and the judicial council represents the judicial branch.

The pastor of a small rural CME church usually lived in a nearby city and sometimes had to travel a long distance to the church. When he lived far away, he would travel to the town where the church was located the Saturday before Sunday services and stay overnight in the home of a church member. He wasn't paid very much and couldn't afford public lodging if public lodging was available. Church members took turns preparing meals for the pastor.

I remember quite clearly one Sunday in particular when my mother prepared dinner for the pastor. She served fried chicken, rice and gravy, green beans, biscuits, and peach cobbler. The biscuits, for some reason, were especially good. Needless to say, it was late afternoon, and I was hungry. All I could think about was how hungry I was and that we had an extra mouth at the table. When we had almost finished dinner and I was still hungry, I noticed there was one biscuit left on the platter. I had my eye on that biscuit. I wanted and needed that biscuit. What was the preacher thinking? Apparently, the preacher was thinking the same thing. We both reached for the biscuit at the same time. I was quicker! I grabbed it with lightning speed. Man, was I happy! That was the best biscuit I had ever eaten. My mother gave me a mean look but I didn't care. I was expecting her to say something about it after the pastor left, but she didn't. When I think about that now, I find it amusing.

Another thing that happened that was church related that I find amusing involved my baby brother. One Sunday, when the ushers passed the collection plates to take up tithes and offerings, my baby brother (he was age four) got up and passed his cap around until my mother stopped him. The church members laughed about it and told my mother to let him keep the money they gave him. When we stopped at the store on the way home, he had collected enough money to buy some ice cream and cookies and had some left over to save.

My mother was very religious, and unless you were sick or indisposed, you went to church every first and third Sunday. She strongly believed in God and the power of prayer. Many nights long after I had gone to bed, I could hear her pray. She prayed aloud, and I heard every word. She would always thank God for waking us up each morning in good physical health with a sound mind. She would give God thanks for our peace of mind, wisdom, knowledge, and understanding. She also thanked God for any money, food, clothing, shelter, family, and friends we had. She would ask him for forgiveness of our sins and His continuing to strengthen us physically, mentally, and spiritually. If anybody in the family got sick, she asked God to make us well and to give us a speedy recovery. Without fail, she always prayed that God would watch over my siblings and me and keep us safe from harm and danger. She prayed that we stay in school and get a good education. When ending her prayer, she would always say, "Dear God, when it's all said and done, let me lay my head upon your breast and breathe my life out sweetly there. When my life on this old earth is over, I hope and pray you have prepared a place for me in your kingdom and you will say a 'Job well done, my good and faithful servant.'"

After I moved to Birmingham, I would visit my mother once or twice a month. Each and every time I visited my mother in Montgomery and I prepared to return to Birmingham, she would always say to me, "Don't forget to pray."

My mother enjoyed singing. To my surprise, she could sing quite well. Apparently, this was a talent she inherited from her father. She often took the lead singing hymns during Sunday morning church service. Also, she would often sing old spirituals when she worked in her vegetable gardens. One of her favorite spirituals was "Amazing

Grace." I enjoyed listening to her sing it. She sang it with a lot of sincerity and feeling. The words of the song, I'm sure, reminded her of God's grace and mercy. As I type this manuscript, I can picture her in my mind singing these four stanzas:

Amazing grace! How sweet the sound,
That saved a wretch like me.
I once was lost, but now I'm found,
Was blind, but now I see.

'Twas grace that taught my heart to fear,
And grace my fears relieved;
How precious did that grace appear
The hour I first believed.

Through many dangers, toils and snares,
I have already come.
'Tis Grace has brought me safe thus far,
And grace will lead me home.

When we've been there ten thousand years,
Bright shining as the sun.
We've no less days to sing God's praise
Than when we first begun.

Many spiritual songs are quite prosaic and poetic. Some of the most beautiful prose and poetry in the world are found in the form of songs in hymnals from which choirs and we as individuals sing every Sunday morning. The words in many spiritual songs, if we would only pay attention, provide many things we can do to live a better life and be a better person. I've incorporated words from the following song in my daily prayer:

"Father, Lead Me Day by Day"

Father, lead me day by day

Ever in Thine own sweet way;
Teach me to be pure and true;
Show me what I ought to do.

When I'm in danger, make me brave,
Make me know that Thou can save;
Keep me safe by Thy dear side;
Let me in Thy love abide.

When I'm tempted to do wrong,
Make me steadfast, wise, and strong;
And when all alone I stand,
Shield me with Thy mighty hand.

It seemed to me that because my mother was very religious, she was a strict disciplinarian. And if she was a Christian, and I believe she was, she was the meanest one I knew. If she told you to do something and you didn't do it quick enough, you got a whipping. If you looked straight into her eyes and gave the impression you didn't want to do what you were told to do, that was perceived by her as contempt and you got a whipping. If a neighbor told her you were disrespectful or did something you shouldn't have done, you got a whipping (this is the way things were in black neighborhoods back then and is probably how the adage "It takes a village to raise a child" originated). If you went on an errand and you didn't return quick enough, you got a whipping. This was child abuse, and in my opinion, she was just too doggone mean. I'm sure my mother had no idea the psychological effect these whippings may have had on my siblings and me. We had to be exceptionally strong mentally to have had any self-esteem when we became adolescents and adults.

When I turned age twelve, I decided "no more whippings." So one day, when my mother attempted to whip me for something for which I felt I didn't deserve a whipping, I grabbed her and held her in a bear hug. I emphatically told her I was tired of being whipped for no good reason and that she needed to stop. When I released her, I made a quick exit. She used a few expletives I don't care to repeat. Afterward, things did get better and life was a little more pleasant. When I became an adult and reminded her how mean she was, she would immediately and emphatically say, "It kept you out of jail." I don't think I was destined to go to jail. However, I could see my mother sincerely thought she did the right thing because in her mind, the whippings kept my siblings and me from going astray and kept us on the right path.

My mother read the Bible every day and encouraged my siblings and me to read it every day as well. Several of my favorite Bible verses are found in Matthew chapter 5 as follows:

> Blessed are the poor in spirit: for theirs is the kingdom of heaven.
> Blessed are they that mourn: for they shall be comforted.
> Blessed are the meek: for they shall inherit the earth.
> Blessed are they which do hunger and thirst after righteousness: for they shall be filled
> Blessed are the merciful: for they shall obtain mercy.
> Blessed are the pure in heart: for they shall see God.
> Blessed are the peacemakers: for they shall be called the children of God (verses 1–9).

> Let your light so shine before men, that they may see your good works, and glorify your Father which is in heaven (verse 16).

> Give to him that asketh thee, and from him that would borrow of thee turn not thou away (verse 42).

First CME Church of Lowndesboro, Alabama

Income

My father, by profession, was a chauffeur. When testing for a driver license was implemented, he was covered under the Grandfather Clause. This was a good thing because, due to his illiteracy, he otherwise couldn't have passed the written exam. When we moved to Montgomery, the doctor for whom my father worked paid him a salary of thirty dollars per week. The doctor died about eight years after we moved to Montgomery. Before he passed, I had the pleasure of meeting him and was in his presence three times. He was tall, about six feet four, and slim, with grayish-black hair.

Immediately after the doctor died, my father started working for the doctor's daughter (our employer) and son-in-law. The daughter was relatively tall, about five feet nine inches, somewhat slim with black hair. She was very energetic, gregarious, and outgoing. The son-in-law was about five feet eight inches tall, very thin and pale with gray hair. He was reserved and not very sociable. Without question, the doctor's daughter was in charge of the household and made all the decisions regarding finances, etc.

Initially, my father did some chauffeuring when he started working for the daughter. For some reason, after a few months, the daughter decided she would drive herself. She spent a lot of time away from home and would frequently go and come throughout the day. My father or I would always bring the car up from the garage to the side entrance of the house. The garage was a two-car garage and was not attached to the house. It sat off the driveway on the same side as the house, about twenty feet from the rear of the house. If the weather permitted, my dad or I washed her car every day either before she left the house or when she returned.

The daughter enjoyed entertaining family and friends. At least once a month, she would have friends and members of her garden club come to the house for brunch or lunch. She also enjoyed having friends come to the house periodically for cocktails. She had a gentleman friend she brought to the house for cocktails on a regular basis. Apparently, she had a special interest in him. He was a retired colonel from the Air Force. She would personally pick him up in her car and bring him to the house for cocktails, once or twice a week, during the day while her husband was at work. It appears she was in the lonely hearts club. I believe her husband had a serious health problem and was impotent. The colonel never drove himself to the house. This continued for several years until the colonel died. The colonel died not long after her husband died.

After the colonel died—and to my shock and surprise—she started a close relationship with a much younger woman. I was shocked! I had no idea she was bisexual. This woman had moved to Montgomery from California, and she had a young daughter. All of her living and household expenses were paid by my employer, who also paid for automobile repairs and eventually bought her a new car. Additionally, the lady for whom my dad and I worked hired my younger brother to work for her newfound friend on a part-time basis. He was hired to take care of the yard, do some household chores, wash the car, etc. My employer's relationship with this woman lasted several years. After that relationship, I don't know if she got involved with anybody else because I moved from Montgomery to Birmingham, Alabama, and my father died shortly after I moved. After my father died, she contacted my mother to see if I would be willing to drive to Montgomery on the weekends and work for her. I told my mother to tell her I couldn't do that, and my mother never heard from her again. She died about a year and a half after my father died.

I always received direction from the doctor's daughter and never the son-in-law regarding things they wanted me to do. She was very complimentary of my work. Periodically, she and I would have brief conversations about things we could do to improve the appearance of the yard or the house. We never had conversations about how I was doing in school or discussed my goals and aspirations. Maybe she assumed I didn't have any and that I would follow in my father's footsteps. When my father told her I had made plans to attend college, she told him she didn't know why because it would be a waste of time. Shockingly, when I graduated from college, she had the audacity to ask me to come to work for her full time. She told me she would match the salary the government job paid. I didn't give her job offer any serious thought because I knew there was no future in it for me. I turned it down. I think I can safely conclude that she saw me as just another good, dependable, black employee she had some compassion for and didn't care whether I grew intellectually or accomplished anything of substance in life. She was a friendly person, and when I was in her presence, she was always cordial.

Her relationship with my father was on a different level. She trusted him, and I think he was her confidant. She discussed things with him of a business nature and of a somewhat personal nature also. I know this to be true because he told me. He never shared with me any details of their conversations. Whenever she went shopping (grocery, etc.), my dad would always take the bags inside. Interestingly, he would always take soap and toilet tissue to her bathroom upstairs and would always replace light bulbs in the bathroom and her bedroom that needed replacing. On several occasions when I was working inside the house, I observed that it took him forty-five minutes to an hour to replace one or two bulbs. Because of their close relationship and the trust she exhibited in him, he was very loyal and committed to his work.

My dad and I had very little contact with our employer's husband. Neither of us ever talked with him at length about anything. We would usually see him as he was leaving for work, returning home from work, or coming home for lunch. During the eleven years I worked for his wife and him, not once did I have a conversation with him. I would only see him in passing and would say "Good morning" or "Good afternoon." He was always low-key and maintained a low profile. Regarding his personality, he appeared to be an introvert and a recluse as well. He very seldom walked around in the yard or sat outside. There were plenty places to sit. Several wrought-iron chairs, wrought-iron benches, and concrete benches were strategically placed in the yard. Also, there was a beautiful gazebo in the backyard not far from the house. He didn't engage in any outside activities other than quail or dove hunting and bass fishing with his son. All of his hunting and fishing was done on their private property. I don't believe he had any close friends other than family. I never saw anyone other than family visit him at home. He was in a very respectable profession that with certainty, under normal circumstances, would have required him to be sociable, confident, outspoken, shrewd, subtle, witty, and at times assertive and aggressive.

In my observation of the husband, and when I think about his demeanor, he may have in fact had a serious health problem with which he was preoccupied. My suspicion may have been confirmed by something tragic that happened. My father was at work one Sunday morning and heard a loud *boom* sound. He went inside and asked the maid if she heard anything. She said she did but had no idea from where the sound might have come. She decided to check all the windows and doors, and they were all intact. About thirty minutes later, my father went inside to put the fishing tackle away from Saturday's fishing trip. When he opened the door to the storage room where the guns, hunting equipment, and fishing tackle were kept, he almost fainted. Teeth, bone, hair, and blood were stuck to the backside of the door and on the wall. He immediately went upstairs and told the wife, and to his surprise, she was quite calm and in his words, "Never shed a tear." Based on her reaction and lack of emotion, I'm sure she heard the sound of the gunshot and probably suspected that what happened had indeed happened. He killed himself with a twelve-gauge shotgun. Everything about the suicide was kept quiet.

Several years before her husband committed suicide, she and he lived in her father's house that she inherited. The house sat almost in the center of about one acre of land and was a two-story white wood-framed colonial-style structure sitting on a hill. It had a partial basement that was used mainly for storage and to house the bottom part of the elevator shaft. The house was furnished throughout with valuable antiques. The first floor consisted of a kitchen, breakfast room, formal dining room, huge living room, bathroom, vestibule, library, study and a large storage room. It was equipped with an elevator and also had stairs leading to the second floor. The second floor consisted of three bedrooms, a bathroom, and a study. There were three entrances to the house: the front entrance leading to the vestibule, the side entrance with steps leading to a hallway that ran from the kitchen to the breakfast room and dining room, and the rear entrance with steps leading to the kitchen.

The yard was a combination of flat and rolling terrain. It consisted of a long teardrop driveway, three lawns, a parking lot, two goldfish ponds with water-spewing statuettes, a gazebo, a rose garden, a rectangular-shaped azalea garden with a lawn in the center, and eight huge flower beds consisting of a variety of plants including azaleas, dogwood, redbud, crepe myrtle, ferns, tulips, creeping charlie, violets, and moss-covered stones. The rose garden was a twenty-by-twenty-feet plot enclosed via a chain-link fence. It consisted of a variety of roses of different colors such as The Doctor, Charlotte Armstrong, American Beauty, Antoine Riviore, Bouquet dOr, Madame Jules Bouché, Catherine Mermet, Crimson Glory, Diamond Jubilee, and Etoile De Lyon.

My father was a gifted gardener and was well known by members of garden clubs in and around the Montgomery area. He was so well known and respected as a gardener an article in the local newspaper, "The Montgomery Advertiser," was written about him. Following is a copy of the article and brief excerpt:

The Magic Wand of Robert Hill

T HERE are Magic Wands in the world today, touching the earth and producing beauty, unexampled in the products of the Machine Age. We call those Magic Wands "green thumbs."

Robert doesn't remember just when he started moving the wild lovelies of nature --the dogwood and crabapple, the lilies and phlex, the hydrangeas and the mayapples, the bloodroot and the white violets -- from the country to town. It could have been before that first hunt, when he was 10 years old, before Germany said "Uncle" in 1918.

He may even tell you that "rotten sawdust" is one of the secret ingredients used in his successful transplants.

When my father wasn't driving (running errands or checking on our employer's property), he was a handyman. He helped take care of the yard, which mostly involved planting flowers and shrubs and hauling several hundred yards of pine straw from Butler County to place around the shrubs and flowers in the flower gardens. Also, he did some household chores such as cleaning the fireplace, polishing furniture, silver, and brass. He was also responsible for waxing the hardwood floors. Additionally, he was expected to do any necessary light carpentry and landscaping work that he could do to help maintain the various properties. Property that our employer owned was located in and outside the Montgomery area.

My father was on call 24/7. Therefore, he was provided transportation (vehicle and gas) to get to and fro, as he frequently had to make trips in and out of town directly from home. He worked from 7:00 a.m. to 5:00 p.m. Monday thru Friday, 7:00 a.m. to 12:00 p.m. on Saturday, and from 6:30 a.m. to 8:30 a.m. on Sunday. On Saturdays, twice a month, our employer and her husband would have supper with their son and his family. They lived about twenty miles north of Montgomery. My father would work as usual from 7:00 a.m. to 12:00 p.m. and then drive them to their son's house. They would return to Montgomery around 10:00 p.m. He was paid an extra ten dollars.

My mother worked about two years as a cleaning lady at the office of a doctor who was a friend of the doctor for whom my father worked. She rode the city bus to and from work. After the doctor for whom she worked died, she was basically a homemaker. She quickly realized that she needed to do something to replace the income she no longer had. She would fry fish (mullet) and sell it on the weekends. This quickly turned into a successful business venture. She also started selling hotdogs, sodas, and sweet-potato pie that you could buy by the slice or the whole pie. To make this business venture even more attractive, she started playing popular music on a phonograph we owned. Our yard on the weekends (Friday evening or Saturday afternoon) usually turned into a party place for the neighborhood kids and some adults. The turnout was constantly good, and everybody had lots of fun eating and dancing. This was my mother's most profitable business venture.

My mother was rather industrious, which seemed to have been an inherent trait. She was quite a resourceful individual as well. She knew that most of the older people in the neighborhood were from Lowndes County and they liked "sour dirt." This was clay dirt with a high concentration of acid that gave it a sour taste. The high acid content turned the clay a light-gray color. She decided this could be another source of income. She started selling it ranging from a nickel for a small chunk to one dollar for a large chunk. The place where we got the dirt was in the Lowndesboro area on property owned by some folk with whom my parents were acquainted. We used a pick to get the dirt and usually got enough to fill one fifty-pound burlap feed bag. This amount of dirt would supply my mother's customers for about three months. She had a number of regular customers, and all the dirt she sold was 100 percent profit.

Out of curiosity, I decided to eat some. It tasted okay. The taste was similar to a dill pickle. I didn't like the gritty residue it left in my mouth. When my mother started selling it, I didn't think much about why people ate it or why they started eating it in the first place. Evidently, it was safe to eat because I never observed or heard of anybody getting sick from eating it. I'm sure it had no nutritional or medicinal value. I think somebody, somewhere, somehow, either accidentally or experimentally tasted the dirt and liked the taste of it and the word got out. I wouldn't eat any today and certainly wouldn't encourage anybody to try it.

She didn't stop with the sour dirt; she had another idea. Since we had two pecan trees and several fruit trees in the yard, she saw the pecans and the fruit from the fruit trees as another opportunity to make some money. Some pecans she sold, some she used for pies and cakes, and some she would keep just for us to eat. Sometimes she would roast a few in the oven. The pecans, year after year, were excellent, and my mother consistently got a good price for them.

The pecan has always been a popular nut and has always been in high demand especially for its many culinary uses. Pecans are grown commercially and are used in a number of food products such as candy, ice cream, cookies, brownies, cereal, cakes, and pies, to mention a few. The pecan, I have learned, is in the walnut family. The tree is easily recognized. It has a deeply furrowed bark and compound leaves with nine to seventeen finely toothed leaflets arranged in feather fashion. At maturity, the fleshy hulls of the short-clustered fruits dry, split along suture lines, and separate into four equal sections, freeing the nuts. The nuts have brown, mottled shells, varying greatly in thickness, size, and shape from long cylindrical with pointed apex to short and roundish or intermediate. Presently, Alabama, Georgia, and Mississippi are the most important producers of the pecan nuts.

A lot of the fruit from the plum and peach trees my mom planted was used to make wine. My mother sold the wine for twenty-five to fifty cents a shot, depending on the customer's ability to pay. This was not a lucrative initiative. She didn't sell the wine often enough to make a big profit. The ones who drank the wine liked it and were repeat customers. She always had some on hand if anybody stopped by and wanted to buy some. A lot of the wine she made was shared with family when they came to visit. To my knowledge, none of the neighbors ever had anything negative to say about my mother's business ventures. As a matter of fact, they were very supportive. They knew we were poor and just trying to survive like most everybody else.

My mother thoroughly enjoyed fishing. I heard her say many times that she would rather fish than eat when she got hungry. She was forever ready to go fishing and would fish from dawn to dusk if she could. The longer she could fish, the better. She went fishing as often as she could in nearby farm ponds with friends and neighbors. When she had a really good catch, she would sell some fish to neighbors. Taking her fishing was at the top of my list of things to do when I went home to visit. She raised her own worms with which to fish, and in spring and summer, she made sure she raised enough to sell to neighbors who enjoyed fishing. She sold the worms for a penny each.

As one can see, my mother was very good in identifying and effectuating business opportunities. In my opinion, she was an amazing woman. I can only imagine what she could have accomplished if she had been blessed to have had the education, knowledge, and entrepreneurial opportunities blacks have today. She was a remarkable person.

At age eleven, I worked with my father over the summer doing yard work. The pay I received for several hours work was whatever the folk for whom I worked decided to pay me. I remember receiving a half-dollar for two or three hours' work to three dollars for all day. I saved all the money I made that summer and was able to buy my school clothes, shoes, and books. Books weren't free. I continued to work each summer thereafter and was able to continue to buy all of my school clothes, shoes, books, school supplies and pay school fees.

When I became a teenager, I started working weekends, holidays, and spring break. My average income, high school through four years of college, was fifteen per week. I lived approximately ten miles from work. Before I started driving, I rode my bike to work almost every day during summer, spring, and autumn and quite often got caught in thunderstorms on my way home. Not having anywhere to take shelter from the rain, I just continued to ride wringing wet until I arrived at home. There weren't any service stations or stores where I could go inside out of the rain because I was black. A black male just couldn't idly stand around inside a place of business because there was a fear and suspicious perception that he might steal something or rob the establishment. This suspicion was a noumenon based on skin color.

At age sixteen, I started waiting table and serving dinner at my employer's home on special occasions and holidays. Dinner guests, in addition to their son's family, included a niece and her family and a married couple (the colonel and his wife) who lived across the street (yes, the colonel's wife knew about his infidelity). I also started serving hors d'oeuvres and mixed drinks at cocktail parties. Guests for cocktail parties were usually family, friends, and members of my employer's garden club. Out of curiosity (as teenagers usually are curious), I would occasionally drink a martini primarily because they were at my disposal and readily available. The maid who worked with me at night especially enjoyed the martinis and always looked forward to helping me serve. She served herself almost as often as she served the guests. I served both gin and vodka martinis. The maid drank both, but she preferred the vodka. I didn't have a preference, and one glass of either was all I cared to partake. I never had a desire to go out and buy alcohol to drink, and to this day as an adult, I will only take a drink or two in a social setting where alcohol is served. I guess I am close to being a teetotaler, but not quite. I will usually buy wine, beer, champagne, or liquor to serve guests I have over to my house for various special occasions.

When I worked at night, I was paid ten dollars extra. The extra income allowed me to occasionally help my parents and siblings financially. It also allowed me to periodically buy lunch or snacks for my sisters if they wanted something to eat. It was periodic that I bought lunch or snacks for myself, as I couldn't afford to buy something every day. I ate something only when I could afford to buy my sisters something to eat or if they didn't want me to buy them anything. I was happy to be in a position to share with family the money I earned. Consequently, I was able to sometimes help my sisters with their tuition and books when they were in vocational school. The money I earned allowed me to now and again buy a few foods I always enjoyed but never ate enough of, such as bananas and ice cream. When my mother went grocery shopping and bought bananas and ice cream, which was infrequent, she could only afford to buy just enough for each of us to get one banana and one serving of ice cream.

When I was age fourteen, the neighborhood organized a B baseball team for boys age twelve through fifteen. The age of the boys on the A team ranged from age sixteen and above. Several sandlot teams in the league had A and B teams. I was the pitcher on our B team. I learned to throw the fastball, drop, curveball, drop curve, and the slider. Not bragging, but I had a pretty good strike out rate. Having to pay fees, buy a glove and a light blue cap for the uniform, the extra income came in handy. We couldn't afford to buy manufactured uniforms. Therefore, we had to wear clothes we already owned. To complete the uniform, we wore a white T-shirt, jeans, and any sneakers that we already owned.

Since the coach couldn't afford to help buy food for the players, the extra income also came in handy when it was time to eat. Usually, I had enough money to buy some food, and I was more than thankful. At the baseball fields where we played the games, there was always someone on the grounds selling hotdogs, potato chips, sometimes fish sandwiches, cookies, candy, and soft drinks. Because our games were sandlot and mostly played in rurban and rural areas, food vendors usually sold food and sodas from the beds of their trucks. Some vendors would prepare hotdogs and fish sandwiches on site at the games. All of our games in rural areas were played in cow pastures that had been converted to baseball fields. There were no bleachers to sit on to watch the game. Therefore, spectators usually sat inside their trucks and cars, on the tailgates of trucks, and on the hoods of trucks and cars. Some spectators sat on the ground. When there were some trees nearby, some male spectators would sit in the trees and watch the game.

Cuisine

Before any of my siblings and I were born, my mother would occasionally go small-game hunting with my father. She was a good marksman with a .410 double-barrel shotgun. One autumn afternoon, I think I was four years old, I recall my mother shooting blackbirds when they stopped to roost in a nearby tree. She killed a bunch. As we prepared the birds to be cooked, it was fun plucking the feathers. The birds were dinner for that night. I also remember my mother going fishing a lot. Pintlalla Creek was close to where we lived. Before we moved to Montgomery, the fish she caught in this creek were the only fish we ate.

One of our main meals for dinner quite often was buttermilk, or sweet milk, as we called it, with cornbread and salt pork. My father would sometimes bring home a five-gallon can of sweet milk from the dairy where he worked. My mother would churn the milk to make butter. The milk left after the sweet milk had been churned was the buttermilk. The butter was used mainly for baking cakes and pies. It was also used as a spread to enhance and add flavor to biscuits, cornbread, grits and rice. For butter, we didn't depend totally on the milk my father brought home from the dairy. We also had butter that was gotten from the milk of the Jersey milk cow we owned.

At the dairy where my father worked, the dairy products that were sold were made from milk produced by Holstein milk cows. The Holstein and Jersey, especially the Holstein milk cow, have had a major impact on the United States economy. Therefore, a brief historical synopsis of the two is provided. There are two breeds of Holsteins: black and white and red and white. Today the black and white Holstein is known worldwide as the highest production dairy cow.

Black-and-white Holsteins originated in Europe. This breed of Holsteins is a large black and white animal that can be from mostly black to mostly white, or half and half. In 1621 through 1664, Dutch farmers who settled along the Hudson and Mohawk Rivers brought black-and-white Holsteins with them to the United States, and for many years, these cattle were known as Dutch cattle and were widely known for their milking qualities. American breeders became interested in this breed of Holsteins in the 1830s. The red-and-white breed of Holsteins was introduced in the US between 1869 and 1885. In the US, the black-and-white Holstein is the preferred breed for most dairy farmers. Many of the dairy cows, when their milk production significantly decreases, are sold to meat-processing companies and ground into hamburger meat.

The Jersey is smaller than the Holstein. It is a beautiful brown cow or brown and white but mostly brown with a dark dished face, light muzzle halo, and long-lashed doe-like eyes. It is valued for the high butterfat content of its milk. The Jersey comes from the Channel Islands and is an excellent example of a refined dairy cow. It is slender in the legs and bony along the body. Jersey cattle were brought to the United States in the 1850s. A breed society was formed in the United States in 1868. There is also a Polled Jersey having no horns for which an American breed society was formed in 1895.

Holstein dairy cow   Jersey dairy cow

In early childhood and through early adolescence, I can't remember eating three full meals a day. I was lucky to eat two meals. I occasionally ate a snack in between meals. When I was in elementary and most of junior high school, I never bought a hot lunch in the school lunchroom and very seldom packed a lunch to take to school. The elementary school I attended, first through third grade, was in a rurban area of Montgomery. It had electricity but no running water or natural gas. The classrooms were cooled in the spring via open windows. The teacher used an electric fan. Classrooms were heated in winter via coal burning space heaters. There was no lunchroom. Students ate lunch at their desks or outside on the playground. Milk for lunch was delivered daily by a local milk company. There was no juice or packaged sandwiches or chips available. Since there was no running water, we had girls and boys outhouses for toilets.

It was seldom that my parents had an extra nickel or dime to give my siblings and me to buy a small carton of milk. The one thing I shall always remember about having something to eat for lunch is when my cousin, who was a grade ahead of me (thank God for my cousin), would share his lunch. He always had a lunch. Most of the time he had a piece of fruit (banana, apple, or orange), a peanut-butter-and-jelly sandwich, or Ritz crackers with peanut butter and jelly. Once and one time only, I took a butter-and-sugar biscuit to school for lunch. When it was time to eat lunch, the butter had melted, and most of it was absorbed by the brown paper bag it was in. This was quite embarrassing. Unfortunately, we didn't have any waxed paper or aluminum foil at home in which to wrap the biscuit.

Can you imagine going to school for over seven years and hardly ever having anything to eat for lunch? A hot lunch in the school lunchroom for a long time was something my siblings and I could only dream about. So many days we would be so hungry it just wasn't fair to have to take a lunch break. It was painful to have to sit in the lunchroom and watch most of the other students eat a hot meal or sack lunch. This was emotional and psychological cruelty. Because the food prepared in the lunchroom smelled so good, I would occasionally find myself imagining eating the food and enjoying how good it must have tasted. Sometimes, when I was alone somewhere and wouldn't be seen, I would think about how bad off financially my family was and literally start crying. Interestingly, I never saw any of my siblings get that emotional. Maybe they were a lot stronger and were able to internalize their emotions or they could better accept the reality of being poor.

Before leaving home for school each day, we always ate something for breakfast. For breakfast Monday thru Friday, we had grits, biscuits, an occasional egg, oil sausage, or fried salt pork we called streak of lean. On Saturday, we ate grits, fried salt pork, freshwater fish, or mackerel patties/croquettes, and biscuits with syrup, jelly, or homemade pear preserves (my mother got the pears from a cousin who lived in Lowndesboro and had several pear trees on her property). Breakfast on Sunday usually consisted of grits, oil sausage, streak of lean, smothered chicken or rabbit. We ate rabbit during the fall and winter when hunting season was in. We never had orange juice or any other fruit juice for breakfast. We always had Kool-Aid, sweet water (sugar and water mixed), or homemade lemonade. Occasionally, we did have milk. We never had cold cereal for breakfast and didn't have toast for breakfast until we got electricity and could afford a toaster and sandwich bread. My parents drank Maxwell House Coffee every morning and evening. Their coffee was sweetened with Domino granulated sugar, and instead of cream, they used cooking milk (PET or Carnation).

We seldom had store-bought fresh fruit at home to eat, such as oranges, apples, grapes, or grapefruit. During the Christmas holidays, my mother usually bought some oranges, apples, and a variety of nuts. Also, during the Christmas holidays, the lady for whom my dad and I worked always bought a large box of Red Delicious apples and a large box of navel oranges to make fruit baskets to give to her friends. My dad would always secretly "borrow" a few to take home. Otherwise, most of the fruit we ate was from the apple, peach, fig, and plum trees we had in the yard when these fruits were in season. My mother's favorite fruit was watermelon, and she would buy one as often as she could.

Spending as much time in the country as I did, I had the pleasure and rare opportunity to eat several fruits that I found growing in the wild that not a lot of young people today have eaten or know much about. You could find these fruits along the highways, in fields, on fence lines, and in woodlands. These fruits are the mulberry, persimmon, muscadine, and maypop. The mulberry and persimmon grow on trees; muscadine and maypop grow on vines. A common fruit that grows on vines and grew abundantly in the wild is the blackberry. Plum trees also grew abundantly especially along highways and fence lines. Most of these fruits found in the wild are there because of fruit dropped by birds or seeds of these fruits in bird droppings (poop). Many kids today and some grown-ups know little or nothing about fruits such as the mulberry, muscadine, persimmon, and maypop. All of these fruits, when fully ripe, are quite delicious and nutritious. Following is a brief description of the aforementioned fruits:

- *Mulberry.* The mulberry is a fruit that is dark purple or purplish black that resembles a raspberry in form and size. The fruit is unusually sweet and insipid in flavor. Mulberries are fair sources of vitamin A, riboflavin, niacin, and vitamin C.
- *Muscadine.* The muscadine is in the grape family. The fruit is purple-black or bronze. The skin is somewhat tough, and the berries grow in clusters of three to five berries. The taste of the juice is like a mixture of plum and apple. The muscadine provides a small amount of vitamins A, B, C, and some minerals.
- *Persimmon.* The persimmon is orange in color, global shaped and about the size of a quarter. When ripe, the persimmon has a soft skin and is sweet with a taste similar to a mango. Persimmons are an excellent source of vitamins A and C.
- *Maypop.* The maypop, or passion fruit, is greenish-purple, egg shaped, and is close to the size of a large plum. It has a leathery, thin tough shell with numerous flattened edible seeds surrounded by a soft yellowish juicy pulp with a delicious aroma. It's a good source for vitamin A, vitamin C, calcium, niacin and riboflavin.

Mulberry

Muscadine

Persimmon

Maypop

A beautiful fruit-bearing tree that caught my attention is the chinaberry tree, which was growing wild on one of the lots my parents bought in Montgomery. I feel compelled to mention it because there are some interesting facts about it that's not widely known. This tree in America is mainly grown for shade. Although the fruit of the chinaberry tree is popular with birds, both the fruit and leaves are poisonous for humans. The berry when ripe is yellow. It is round and is about 30 percent larger than a cranberry. The seed is very hard and is about 80 percent of the berry. The wood of the chinaberry tree is considered to be of very high quality. The wood, when made into planks, is relatively immune to fungus growth, warping, and cracking. Before the invention of plastic beads, the hard seeds of the chinaberry tree were often used as beads in the manufacture of necklaces. In Europe, monks have been known to use the seeds to make rosaries. The chinaberry tree in addition to being grown for shade is also grown for ornamental purposes.

Chinaberry tree

Before we got electricity in the neighborhood and could afford a refrigerator, we used an icebox (a refrigerator cooled with ice) to keep perishable foods fresh. The icebox didn't work very well. Therefore, perishable foods had to be eaten within a short timeframe to avoid spoilage. Dry goods such as lard, butter, sugar, flour, salt, pepper, grits, rice, cornmeal, peas, and beans were heavily depended on. The lard and flour were used to make biscuits, cakes, crust for sweet-po-tato pies, peach-and-blackberry cobblers. Lard and flour were also used for frying and for making gravy. Cornmeal was used to make cornbread, dressing, and mush (a thick porridge boiled with water and/or milk). When the mush was ready to be eaten, a little salt and butter were added, which made it quite tasty. This was a good mid-day or late-evening meal.

My father became acquainted with the butcher at the grocery store where our employer shopped. He told the butcher that our employer had some hunting dogs and they would appreciate any beef or pork bones he could give him to feed to the dogs. When my father was given the bones and there was some meat on them, my mother would use them to make soup. My parents, without fail, had several vegetable gardens every year. For dinner, when fresh vegetables were in season, we had a choice of collard, turnip, or mustard greens; butter beans, squash, okra, tomatoes, corn, peas, snap beans, or sweet potatoes.

The sweet potato was one vegetable we were fortunate to have almost year round. When we harvested sweet potatoes during summer, we preserved a large volume of them by building sweet-potato mounds. The mounds were built of dirt (preferably clay), pine straw, and plastic. We found that the best place to build a mound was in the side of a small hill if that was feasible. Putting the mound in the side of a hill was almost equivalent to placing the sweet potatoes in a cave. Hence, the mound was surrounded by solid dirt that helped maintain a good temperature and minimized moisture. Moisture contributed significantly to decay.

For dinner, Monday through Friday, my mother usually cooked cornbread and some kind of vegetable. Pork neck bones, fatback or salt pork was cooked with all vegetables for seasoning and to add flavor. Often, this would be the only meat we ate for dinner. We always had corn bread to eat with vegetables. My mother seldom cooked corn bread in the oven. She usually cooked what we called stove-top corn bread. She would mix corn meal with boiling hot water and stir it adding butter and salt until she got the desired consistency. She would either place all the mixture in the skillet to form a large cake of cornbread or use her hands as a mold to shape some of the mixture in an oval or round form and place it in hot cooking oil(lard) and fry it until medium brown. This bread was delicious.

Fish, when it was available, was served for dinner on Saturday. The fish would be either freshwater fish we caught or fish my mother bought at the grocery store. For Sunday dinner, ninety percent of the time we ate chicken, rice, and a vegetable. On a few occasions when finances permitted, we would have pork chops, pork steak, ham, or roast for Sunday dinner along with rice and a vegetable. During the fall and winter months, we relied heavily on wild game for dinner on Saturday and Sunday more often than not.

The main entrée for Thanksgiving and Christmas dinner was turkey or ham. The folk for whom my dad worked would give us a turkey for Thanksgiving and a ham or Turkey for Christmas. Side dishes were dressing, potato salad, sweet potatoes, and collard greens. For dessert, we had a coconut, pound, or caramel cake and sweet potato pies. Something to drink included water, lemonade, or Kool-Aid.

We raised Rhode Island Red chickens. They were raised mainly for eggs. However, we would occasionally eat one for dinner or breakfast. Rhode Island Reds are somewhat attractive birds. Their feathers are usually rust colored, and their eyes are red-orange; they have yellow feet, and their beaks are reddish brown. Reds are generally raised for meat and eggs. Roosters usually weigh 8.5 pounds and hens 6.5 pounds. Cockerels (young roosters) are about 7.5 pounds and pullets 5.5 pounds. Hens are frequent egg-layers capable of producing over two hundred eggs per year.

Reds are tough birds in terms of heartiness, resistance to illness, and are good at foraging and free-ranging. They are typically docile, quiet, and friendly but can be aggressive when annoyed. Most roosters will attack strangers if they feel nervous or have never seen the intruder. Both roosters and hens can be aggressive toward young children and adults but, if raised properly and lovingly, can be very loving and affectionate. They will come when they see their owner or when called. The Rhode Island Red is the state bird of Rhode Island.

Rhode Island Red Hen

Our neighbors who lived directly behind us on First Street were my cousins, and they raised carrier pigeons. To my knowledge, they raised them for no particular reason other than they just enjoyed raising them. I often noticed that several would fly away throughout the day and later return. Maybe this was their way of exercising, or it was just their nature to spread their wings.

Carrier pigeons are amazing birds. For the benefit of my young readers, I'm sharing some information about the carrier pigeon that I found to be quite interesting. Carrier pigeons historically were used to carry messages. They were used to carry messages during World War I and World War II. Their flying speed could average ninety miles per hour. During the First and Second World Wars, they were used to transport messages back to their home coop behind the lines. When they landed, wires in the coop would sound a bell or buzzer, and a soldier of the signal corps would know a message had arrived. He would go to the coop, remove the message from the canister, and then send it to the right persons by telegraph, field phone, or personal messenger.

Carrier pigeons did an important job that was very dangerous. If enemy soldiers were nearby when a pigeon was released, they knew that the bird would be carrying important messages and tried their best to shoot the pigeon down so the message wouldn't be delivered. Some of the pigeons became quite famous among the infantrymen for whom they worked. One pigeon named the Mocker flew fifty-two missions before he was wounded. Another was named Cher Ami. He was injured in the last week of the war. He lost one of his feet but managed to reach his destination. As a result, two hundred infantrymen were saved.

Since some of my cousin's pigeons had an abiding habit of eating the feed we put out for the chickens, I thought it was only right that we sometimes ate a pigeon or two for dinner. After all, the pigeons were plentiful. I supplied the pigeon. I killed the pigeons with a Daisy pump BB gun. The gun was powerful and quiet enough to get the job done without attracting attention. I always aimed for the head. I never got caught shooting a pigeon. If the pigeon wasn't a squab (a young pigeon about four weeks old), the meat was usually tough. There was quite a difference in eating the meat of a mature pigeon and a young one. The meat of a pigeon that was several years old was usually almost too tough to eat. I'm not sure there is a way to cook it to tenderize it other than the way we cooked it. We found that pot-boiling it, cooking it slowly with low heat, adding white onion, salt, black pepper, and bell pepper was the best way to prepare it. Before I killed a pigeon, I could sometimes (mainly because of its size) determine if it was an old or a young one. Because the meat was somewhat tough and we weren't crazy about the taste, it was infrequent that we had pigeon for dinner. My mother never said anything, but I could sense that she wasn't very happy with my killing our cousin's pigeons. For some reason, and I don't know if it was because I had a guilty conscious, I always felt that my cousin knew I was killing his pigeons. Maybe he didn't care or because he had so many he was glad I killed a few.

I was an excellent marksman with the BB gun. I rarely missed my target. I killed lots of birds with the BB gun. My maternal grandmother was half-Creek Indian, and she would always eat the birds

I killed. She would eat any kind of bird I killed except a blue jay. What was it about a blue jay? I asked why she didn't eat blue jay, and she never gave me a definitive answer, so I just figured she had a good reason. I would shoot birds during the fall and winter when they weren't caring for their young. I mostly killed blackbirds, robins, thrashers, and doves that were foraging in our yard, vacant lots, or open fields. When my grandmother cooked the birds, she fried them slowly in a little lard and butter, adding salt and pepper to enrich the flavor.

Because of something that happened in a situation with me involving the BB gun, let me interject something about gun safety. I went out to shoot some birds for my grandmother one Saturday morning, and when I returned home, the BB gun was empty. I was sure I had used all the BBs. I put the BB gun away where I usually kept it, and without my knowledge, my younger brother reloaded it and used it shortly after I put it away. Some friends came over to my house to play, and while playing I grabbed the BB gun and told one of them I was going to shoot her. I assumed the gun was empty because that's the way I left it. I cocked the gun and pulled the trigger. Thank God I missed her eyeball by a micrometer and the pellet was lodged in the eye socket, where it was easily removed. The message here is that anytime you handle a gun that is not a toy gun, always check it for ammo especially if you are in an environment where it doesn't need to be loaded. Assuming that the gun was empty reminds me of a maxim: "Assumption is the mother of all foul ups."

My grandmother's favorite soda was a RC cola. Her favorite cookie was the Ginger Snap. She enjoyed smoking a pipe. Observing her smoke a pipe, reminded me a lot of her Indian heritage. She always smoked George Washington pipe tobacco. I made her several pipes out of corncobs and bamboo. In making the pipe, I would cut off the bottom part of the corncob ("cob" for short) about one and three quarters of an inch long. I would then hollow out the center of the cob. Next, I would bore a hole in one side of it about one-half inch from the bottom. A piece of bamboo about four and a half inches long, about the size of a no. 2 pencil, was inserted into the hole. The bamboo was the pipe's stem.

The lady for whom my dad and I worked owned property northeast, south, and southwest of Montgomery. The latter property (about forty miles from Montgomery) was the property I visited most of the time because this was where my father spent the majority of his time and where he did his farming. The acreage southwest of Montgomery was approximately five thousand acres. The doctor in Montgomery for whom my father previously worked told him his family paid $0.50 per acre for the land. It was a slave plantation during slavery.

On the property, which was only a few feet off one of the dirt roads that ran through the place, on the top of a small hill, sat a white three-bedroom, wood-framed house. This house was where the folk for whom we worked stayed when they came down to visit and to go hunting or fishing. In addition to the three bedrooms, the house consisted of a living room, sitting room, dining room, kitchen, and bathroom. The house was fully furnished. The only public utility it had was electricity. It had running water that was supplied by an electric water pump. Electric heaters were used for heat in winter and electric fans were used to keep cool in summer. For cooking, there was a gas stove that used butane gas. The house had two porches, one at the front entrance facing the road and the other, which was a partial wraparound porch, extending from the sitting room on the west side of the house to the kitchen on the north side.

My father and I were responsible for maintaining the yard and keeping the house clean. When we had a lot to do and decided to go coon hunting, my father and I would stay overnight. We slept in the smallest bedroom with the understanding that the other two were off-limits. My father was overseer of the property, and he would check on the place and tenant farmers once or twice per week.

Some of the land on the place was leased by tenant farmers who did some farming, raising livestock and fowl. When my father found the time, he did some farming. The plow was the main tool for planting. To prepare the soil for planting, my dad used what is called a walking plow. This plow had interchangeable blades for plowing and was pulled by a horse named Louise. This was the horse my parents owned when we lived in Lowndes County that they decided to keep. One blade for the plow, I recall, was used primarily for tilling the soil, and another one was used for making rows for planting. A third blade was small and narrow and was used to open the middle of the rows for planting the seeds. Once the seeds were planted, my father used a harrower to smooth the soil and cover the seeds. The vegetables he grew were tomatoes, corn, sweet potatoes, squash, and crowder peas.

Besides small-scale farming, my dad raised goats and hogs. He also raised Rock Cornish chickens for the people for whom we worked. He always kept a few for himself, of course. They were raised for meat only. If you have never eaten goat, you are missing a treat. Generally, goat is tender and more delicate in taste than lamb. The goat is relatively small when compared to the Hog. The goat dressed out weighed about twenty-five to thirty pounds. The hog dressed out weighed about eighty to one hundred pounds.

Hogs were raised mostly for ham, bacon, chitterlings, and lard for cooking. Unlike hogs, goats were slaughtered any time of the year because they were much smaller and more quickly eaten. Hogs, traditionally, were slaughtered in winter because there was a lot more meat that had to be kept for a much longer period of time, and cold weather was the best time to preserve it. Winter was the best time because the outside temperature, if you were lucky, was either at freezing, slightly above or below. Since we didn't have sufficient refrigeration to keep the meat fresh, it was heavily packed away with salt for curing or smoked with hickory chips and then packed away with salt. The meat was stored in the crib or a special built smoke house. Salt preserved the meat and kept it from spoiling.

In addition to other duties, my father trained bird dogs that were kept on the place in Butler County. He trained five bird dogs: two English Setters named Bob and Rex, a Gordon Setter named Troy, and two Pointers named Ben and John. The doctor for whom my father worked didn't prefer a particular breed. He liked owning a variety. He enjoyed hunting with either breed as they were well trained. A description of each breed follows:

- *English Setter.* The English Setter has a long head, hanging ears, a deep chest, and pointed tail. Its coat is longer on the ears, chest, legs, and tail. It may be all white, black-and-white or tricolored (black, white, and tan), or white-flecked with a darker color. Bob's coat was tricolored, and Rex's coat was white and lemon.
- *Gordon Setter.* The Gordon Setter has a soft, wavy coat that is black with tan on the head, throat, chest, and legs.
- *Pointer.* The pointer has a long muzzle, hanging ears, tapered tail, and a short, smooth coat. The coat is usually white with black, liver-colored, yellowish-brown, or reddish-brown markings. Ben's coat was white with black markings. John's coat was white with liver-colored markings.

When my father trained and worked the bird dogs, I would kill five or six quail. Therefore, we occasionally had a few quail to eat. The quail is a beautiful brown-and-white bird and is fun to hunt. When my mother cooked quail, she split them open down the back, dipped them in melted butter, sprinkled them with salt and pepper, and placed them in a pan in the oven. She added a little water and melted butter in the bottom of the pan and cooked the quail for about thirty minutes. The taste of the quail was quite savory and delicious.

My father trained and worked bird dogs during early fall when, hopefully, snakes weren't very active and had begun hibernating. When the dogs pointed a covey of quail and the quail were flushed, I would kill a few. Killing quail wasn't easy. I quickly learned that to kill a quail, you had to single one out in the covey. It didn't matter that you were using a shotgun. You couldn't just shoot into the covey and kill a bunch of quail.

Quail was considered a delicacy, and quail hunting was considered a white man's sport. Had I been caught shooting quail, my dad and I both might have been fired. I didn't shoot any quail unless my father was for certain it was safe to do so. Had I been caught, however, I think I could have convincingly said I killed a few to train the dogs. I didn't shoot quail every time we worked the dogs because that would have fractured the coveys and scattered the birds too much. To ensure that there were plenty quail to hunt, my father and I put out bird feeders. Throughout the year we kept them supplied with birdseed.

Let me tell you how I learned to kill quail. When my dad and I went quail hunting to work the dogs, he was responsible for controlling the dogs and giving them commands. Therefore, he thought it was a good idea for me to do the shooting especially my first time going with him. Unknown to me, he decided he would have some fun. He knew exactly what I would do, as he had not given me any advice on shooting quail. Sure enough, I did exactly what he expected. When the dogs pointed and the birds were flushed, I shot directly into the covey at least twice and didn't kill a single bird. My dad pretended he was shocked and perplexed. I was certainly shocked. After all, I used a Remington twelve-gauged shotgun and the shells had lots of pellets. I told my dad I thought something was wrong with the shells and decided to examine them because I knew I should have killed at least four or five birds. After a good laugh, he told me that there is a simple technique to killing quail. He said what I needed to do is visually pick one bird out in the covey and then shoot it. The next time I did exactly what he told me to do, and that's when I learned how to kill quail.

When I wasn't hunting or doing chores in the house or yard, I looked forward to going fishing. There were three large fishponds on the place. They were stocked with largemouth bass and shellcracker, a sunfish that's common in farm ponds in the South. I had lots of fun catching shellcracker when they were spawning in spring and summer. It was easy to catch twenty or thirty in less than an hour. I mostly used red worms and earthworms for bait. I frequently found plenty worms to fish with in damp places under leaves and from cow and horse manure. I also had lots of fun catching bass especially when I used artificial lures. Using artificial lures to catch bass took finesse, patience, and technique. My favorite lures for catching largemouth bass were the "purple plastic worm," "white rooster tail," and "silver spoon." The fishing tackle and lures I used, of course, were owned by the folk for whom my dad and I worked.

Speaking of fishing, one spring morning, I was fishing for bass in one of the ponds using live minnows and I caught a five pounder. We weighed the fish at the country store where we usually stopped to buy gas. This was a big bass, and I was really excited. I was thirteen years old, and I had done something my dad and older brother hadn't done. I took the bass to show it off to my father, who was plowing in the sweet-potato field. He was excited for me. I put the fish in the refrigerator until we left to head home.

On the way home, my father decided he would give the bass to the man for whom we worked. What could I say? What could I do? I was appalled, highly disappointed, and somewhat baffled. Initially, I couldn't quite understand why he would consider giving my trophy fish to somebody. Of course, all we would have done was eat it because we couldn't afford to have it mounted. After thinking for a while about my dad's decision, I concluded that maybe this was a way for him to stay in his employer's good grace or to show gratitude for his job or for something his employer had done for him. They ate the fish for dinner the next day and told my father they thoroughly enjoyed it. He was pleased. I was still a little perplexed about the whole thing but at the same time happy my dad was pleased.

When we didn't have freshwater fish at home to eat, my mother would buy mullet when she went grocery shopping. I think mullet was the cheapest saltwater fish she could buy. When it was fried and seasoned with salt and pepper or eaten with hot sauce, it was delicious. Occasionally, she would buy Spanish mackerel. She always brought home several large fifteen-ounce cans of mackerel. She used the mackerel to make mackerel patties and croquettes. Mackerel patties were quite tasty when served with hot buttered biscuits and syrup or eaten with hot buttered rice.

Another abundant food source was wild game, such as rabbit, squirrel, opossum, and raccoon. I thoroughly enjoyed hunting rabbit and squirrel. Now that I am in my senior years, I don't get to hunt much anymore. Fortunately, I have a cousin in Montgomery who likes to rabbit hunt and I go rabbit hunting with him occasionally.

Hunting nowadays is nothing like it was when I was growing up. The hunting climate and places to hunt small game are quite different. It's rare to find someone who hunts rabbit, squirrel, opossum, or raccoon. Today, deer hunting is the most popular in the South and is rather widespread in the US. Quail and dove hunting, except on private property and hunting preserves, is practically nonexistent. The guns I used for hunting small game when I was growing up were a twelve-gauge and twenty-gauge Remington pump, and a .410 double-barrel Remington. These guns, owned by the man for whom my dad and I worked, were available to us to use whenever we went hunting.

We didn't own a rabbit dog, so when I went rabbit hunting, I had to find the rabbit myself and flush it out of its bed or hiding place. When we went squirrel hunting, though, we had a squirrel dog with which to hunt. He was light brown, and his name was Rusty. Rusty was part feist and cur and, to this day, the best squirrel dog with which I've ever hunted. Rusty was owned by the people for whom my dad and I worked. On any given day, we could easily kill twelve to fifteen squirrels in two to three hours. Squirrels were plentiful.

The squirrels that we hunted were the western gray squirrel and the fox squirrel. The gray squirrel mostly nested in oak, hickory, and hackberry trees and usually constructed its nest using leaves, bark, and small branches. The nests are placed high in trees and are large and bulky. Both the gray and fox squirrels eat acorns, pinecones, nuts, bark, fruit, berries, fungi, and insects and spend some time foraging on the ground.

The fox squirrel is larger than the gray and is the largest tree squirrel. Its coat is typically reddish brown with a lighter belly. The fox squirrel goes through three different color phases—gray over yellow, reddish brown, and black. Color variations may include white markings with white on face and white tip of tail, white ears, white nose, and black head. The tail is usually mixed colors except in the black color phase. Bottoms of feet are black, and the tail is bushy and often has yellow tips on tail hairs. In the South, fox squirrels prefer to nest in tall pine trees, which provide excellent camouflage. The fox squirrel, unlike the gray, is a bit more adventurous and enterprising as it may change location in the fall. The fox will use nests in summer and tree cavities in winter. It also spends a lot more time foraging on the ground and moves much faster and with greater agility.

Fox Squirrel

Hunting raccoon ("coon hunting" to hunters) was my father's favorite pastime. He loved coon hunting, and he loved his coon dogs. He, at one time or another, owned four coon dogs: Bill, a Redtick or English coonhound; Herbert, a Treeing Walker; and George and Sam, both Black and Tan. Of the four coonhounds, my father's favorite was Herbert. Coon hunters usually have a particular breed of coonhound they prefer because of the hound's physical characteristics and hunting style. Each coon hunter always held his hound in high regard as to hunting ability, as did my father. His hound, just as any other coon hunter's hound, was always the best of the best, and there was a lot of bragging. Owning a good coonhound was prestigious. To give you a clear picture of the differences in coonhounds that I believe you will find quite interesting, I have provided the following general information on each breed of hound my dad owned.

- *Redtick/English.* The color is predominantly red with white-red or white-lemon spots. Bill's coat was red with white-red spots. The coat of the Redtick is hard, medium length, and dense. This breed has a deep, broad chest; strong, slightly arched back, slightly domed skull; medium stop, square muzzle; large open nostrils; and dark eyes set wide apart. Ears hung a little low with fine texture and soft feel. The tail is medium length with slight brush carried gaily. Feet are compact and well padded. In the field, the Redtick possesses tremendous track drive and opens on first scent. It barks freely while trailing game. Also, it has a tremendously effective nose and will work all types of tracks including cold trails. It is not friendly around the tree (this hound by nature doesn't like competition) and will stand its ground once it has decided the game is there. Because of its tenacity and fast tracking ability, the Redtick is a very successful hunter.

- *Treeing Walker.* The coat is tricolored (white, black, and tan) with white or black being the predominant color. Herbert's coat was tricolored with black being the dominant color. The Treeing Walker's coat is smooth, hard, and close. This breed has a moderately long, muscular back with broad and slightly arched loins. The head is carried well up, and the skull is broad and full. The eyes are dark and set well apart. This hound has medium-length ears set moderately low and slightly round at the tip. The tail is strong at root, set high and curved up and forward. Feet are solid, compact, and catlike. Like the Redtick, the Walker is also well liked by night hunters. This hound is very independent and has a competitive nature. He/she possesses speed and stamina and has an uncanny gaminess in locating, tracking, and treeing game. The voice of this hound is a brawl or chop on the trail with a good changeover to a resounding chop on the tree. Some walkers open freely on the trail, while others possess the ability to "drift" a track as they bark occasionally, although never in the same place, until they tree their game. Many Walkers also have scenting ability to tree "layup" coons that haven't been on the ground in some time.

- *Black and Tan.* The color is a coal black with rich tan markings. Both George and Sam's coat were predominantly black, but George's coat had more brown than Sam's. The Black and Tan's coat is short and dense, and this breed of hound has a deep chest with long and strong limbs. Its neck is muscular, and it has well-developed flews, hazel to dark-brown eyes, large black round nose, with low-set long ears hanging in folds. The tail is strong and carried high almost perpendicular to its back when tracking. Many Black and Tans possess great speed and are used primarily for coon hunting. Their short, tough coats enable them to withstand the rigors of thick cover as well as cold swamps. Their voice is a deep, melodious brawl when running a track. They are bred to be open trailers on track and be hard, pressure tree dogs. They are accurate tree dogs and seem to resist the temptation to pull to other running hounds once they end their track.

We hunted coons at night during the fall and winter and caught plenty. Hunting at night was a challenge. Though we used flashlights and kerosene lanterns for light, visibility was limited. Occasionally, the person walking in front of you would inadvertently release a small tree branch that would hit you in your face or you would trip over a log or tree stump and fall sometimes head first in briars or mud. Sometimes, the terrain where we hunted coons was rugged—steep hills, slopes, boulders, creeks, and thick undergrowth. All of this was a part of coon hunting, and at the end of the hunt, it was all about doing something we enjoyed doing.

When we were hunting and the hounds were on a cold trail, we would build a fire and just sit around the fire for a while and eat peanuts, pecans, crackers, cheese, potted meat, or Vienna sausage. While sitting around the fire, I enjoyed listening to the old-timers tell ghost stories and tales about their coon-hunting experiences. I also enjoyed listening to the hounds work the coon and tree it. You could tell by the hound's bark if a trail was hot or cold. There was also a difference in the bark when a coon was treed. The bark was almost nonstop, with an occasional howl depending on the breed of hound. When we found the tree the coon was in, we would find the coon with a flashlight and, most of the time, shoot it out of the tree to get it. To give the hounds an opportunity to see a live coon up close and to reinforce their hunting skills, we would sometimes make the coon come down the tree or jump out of it by making a lot of noise hollering and tapping on the tree with sticks.

I enjoyed skinning the coons we caught. I skinned a lot of coons, and I was quite skilled at it. The secret to skinning a coon was a sharp pocketknife. I knew I had done an excellent job if the entire skin was intact when I finished. Using my small pocketknife that I kept razor sharp, I would make a subcutaneous incision from the bottom of the mouth, down the neck, out and up each front leg, then down the belly, out and up each hind leg. I would cut off the feet and tail and leave them attached to the hide. We saved a few hides to train coonhound pups.

When my mother cooked a coon, she would cut it in four quarters (head removed); season it with salt, pepper and white onion; put it in a large pot, covering it with water; and slow-cooked it with moderate heat until done (this ensured tenderness). She removed it from the pot and placed it in a roaster without the top, then she added barbecue sauce and baked with medium heat until a thin crust was formed. When my mother cooked goat, it was prepared the same as coon. Because the goat is a much larger animal, most parts of the goat were cooked individually. Squirrel was pot-boiled only and also seasoned with salt, pepper, and white onion. Rabbit was either fried or smothered using the same seasonings and served with gravy. My mother's favorite wild-game dish was baked opossum and sweet potatoes.

My mother made her own barbecue sauce. She used a mixture of tomato ketchup, tomato paste, honey, molasses, brown sugar, mustard, apple cider vinegar, and fresh lemons. She sliced several lemons and placed them in a boiler with the other ingredients and cooked them slowly on top of the stove stirring often until the lemons were soft.

On Friday of each week, my father would pick up discarded bread and pastries from a local bakery. The doctor for whom my dad worked had an agreement with the bakery owner that my father would collect the discarded items each week. Many of these items were shared with neighborhood kids and mixed with dog food and fed to our dogs and the bird dogs my dad trained. Before the bread was fed to the dogs, I sorted through it to pick out any that wasn't molded that I thought would be fit to eat. I usually didn't find much. Once, I pulled out some doughnuts I thought were fresh enough to take to school for lunch. I was in the fifth grade. I took the doughnuts to school and was shocked when I opened the bag to eat one. It was so stale I could barely break it. I put it in the trash, and it was just another day of school without lunch. Many days I would be so hungry it was pure torture to sit in the lunchroom and smell the aroma of the food that had been cooked. Most of the kids who didn't have anything to eat for lunch were kids who rode the school bus with me.

Two food items my family and I ate that I would be remiss not to mention are what we called lye corn (hominy) and crackling cornbread. To make lye corn, my mother would place a certain amount of hard, dried whole-kernel shelled corn in the wash pot we kept outside and let it soak overnight in measured amounts of water, lye, and ashes from wood burned in the stove and fireplace. The water, lye, and ashes formed a strong alkaline solution that would cause the husk of the corn to soften, and when the corn was boiled, the husk would pop open, freeing the pulp. The pulp was removed from the pot and placed in cool water. After the pulp cooled, it was thoroughly washed and put in a large pan. The lye corn was prepared for eating by placing it in a large skillet, adding salt, black pepper, butter, and just enough water to keep the corn from sticking to the skillet. Crackling cornbread was cornbread made with fried pork skins (cracklings). When a hog was butchered, skin from certain parts of the hog was fried to get lard. Lard was a very important product because it was widely used by blacks for frying a variety of foods such as eggs, chicken, small game, liver, ham, pork chops, steak, and fish.

*****

We Thank Thee, O God

We thank thee, o God,
For the gifts thou hast given,
The blessings thou hast bestowed;
Thy goodness and mercy our tongues would recite.

We thank thee, o God,
For all things thou hast made,
Our senses, our souls to delight;
The beauties and glories that greet us by day and by night.

We thank thee for love, that most wonderful gift,
For friendships and fellowships dear;
For all the enjoyment and pleasures they yield,
For home with its gladness and cheer.

Medical Care And Physical Fitness

My parents, siblings, and I never had a problem with being over-weight. Almost everything we did involved some form of physical activity. We did a lot of walking most of the day every day. We had no health, vision, or dental insurance. My siblings and I saw a doctor or dentist only if there was an emergency. If anyone in the family got sick, a home remedy was used first. Some home remedies seemed to have worked okay, and some didn't. When winter came, my siblings and I were given cod-liver oil on a regular basis. My mother got the cod-liver oil from the doctor for whom she worked. If we caught a cold, we also took castor oil.

I recall at least three of my siblings and me having had several childhood diseases such as measles, chicken pox, and mumps. I dreaded mumps the most. You didn't want the mumps! The home remedy for mumps was a sardine compress tied underneath your chin. Can you imagine having to wear a sardine compress? This was disgusting and most definitely child abuse to the tenth degree. There is no way I would have subjected my children or anybody else's to such an inhumane home remedy. Kids today should thank God for modern-day medicine.

In my early teens, I remember my mother and I talking about childhood diseases. She told me that I had rheumatic fever when I was quite young. Since she didn't tell me much about it and I was seemingly healthy at the time, I didn't ask her any questions. However, after I became an adult and was diagnosed with hypertension, mitral valve prolapse (MVP), and an enlarged heart, I thought about rheumatic fever and wondered about its effects. I did some research and learned that it can cause cardiac involvement, such as heart murmurs, increased heart rate, heart enlargement, inflammation of the heart muscle, contracture of the heart valves, and inflammation of the joints. The symptoms, severity, and aftereffects of rheumatic fever are highly variable, ranging from a condition so mild as to go unnoticed, to a severe acute attack associated with cardiac failure and death. To control the high-blood pressure, pain, and malfunctioning of the mitral valve, I was prescribed medication that I have continued to take.

As if it was not enough to have hypertension, MVP, and an enlarged heart, I also learned that I had a problem with high LDL (bad) cholesterol. This condition was discovered while undergoing tests for chest pain affiliated with MVP. After extensive testing, it was determined that the high LDL was attributed in part to heredity, which made it more difficult to get the LDL and HDL (good cholesterol) numbers where they should be. With continuous medication (several different ones), a low-fat diet, and having to deal with excruciating side effects (severe muscle and joint pain) from medication, I wasn't able to get the numbers down and maintain them at a desirable level. To get some relief from the side effects, I had to periodically stop taking medicine for several weeks and then start taking it again. This stop-and-start process of taking cholesterol lowering medication continued for over twenty-five years, and I was never able to get the bad cholesterol under control.

Consequently, on October 1, 2010, I had a second heart attack and was hospitalized. I previously had a light heart attack in 1985. An arteriogram was done on October 4 to check the condition of my arteries. The results were shocking. Five of my arteries were partially blocked, ranging from 50 percent to 90 percent. My main artery was 90 percent blocked. I had open heart, quadruple bypass surgery on October 6. The surgeon had planned to do five bypasses, but because my sternum was so arthritic, they had difficulty cutting through it and couldn't keep me under anesthesia long enough to do five. The surgery was a success.

I am on a low-fat diet and still taking medication to try and regulate LDL cholesterol. All of my siblings have high cholesterol and are on medication to try and control it. Additionally, all of my siblings and I have health issues involving the gastrointestinal tract of the digestive system that doctors have attributed to heredity. Two main health issues are diverticulitis and the propensity for polyps to develop in the colon. As a result of these health issues, four of my siblings and I have had colon surgery. My surgery was done on August 14, 2012. Half of my colon was removed.

When I was age twelve, one summer afternoon, I was playing barefooted outside in the yard and stepped on a rusty nail that was sticking through a board lying in the yard. To remove the nail, which was in my left foot, I stepped on the board with my right foot while I pulled my left foot up removing the nail. Not knowing how dangerous a puncture like this could be, I assumed it would heal and I would be okay. A few days later, my foot started aching and swelling. I told my mother about the swelling, and out came the home remedy. She tied a steak compress, which was supposed to draw the bacteria out, to the bottom of my foot. This didn't work. My foot continued to swell to about the size of a soft ball.

One Sunday night in August, around 9:00 p.m., the pain got so severe I literally started crying. My head was throbbing. The poison had gotten well into my bloodstream. I was in so much pain my father rushed me to the hospital emergency room. The doctor immediately prepped my foot and cut it open, making an incision replicating a cross. I didn't know it could feel so good to be cut. I could feel the poison draining out of my body. The doctor told me if I had been one hour later getting to the hospital, I would have contracted lockjaw (an early symptom of tetanus characterized by spasm of the jaw muscles and inability to open the jaws). He wrote me a prescription for an antibiotic and gave me a tetanus shot. In about six weeks, my foot had healed.

When I enrolled in college and started taking classes, I would often go to school without eating breakfast and, most of the time, wouldn't eat anything until late in the day. Each day, as soon as my last class for the day was over, I immediately went to work. Occasionally, I would eat lunch with my elder sister, who lived near the campus. During the first semester of my sophomore year, because of the constant pressure I put on myself to arrive at school and work on time and frequently not eating, I developed a peptic ulcer. The pain affiliated with a peptic ulcer is a constant hurting and burning sensation in a localized area. The burning sensation comes from the acid that's secreted in the stomach.

I told my father about the constant stomach pain. Since we couldn't financially afford to pay a doctor and pay for the necessary medical tests that had to be done, he told our employer. Without hesitation, she sent me to her family doctor and paid all the expenses. I am eternally grateful. I thanked her, and I thanked God. Up to the time she passed away, she always said she saved my life. This may be true. I didn't get upset about it because I got the medical treatment I needed and I was able to concentrate and focus on my studies. I never felt obligated or felt that I owed her anything extra because my father and I worked long hours for which we were underpaid and we both did an excellent job. We both had a strong work ethic. We were always at work ahead of schedule and frequently stayed longer than required.

Having grown up poor, watching my parents struggle and noticing how hard they worked to make ends meet, I decided long before I became an adolescent that if I were going to accomplish something in life, I had to work hard and always do my best. The summer leading into my junior year of college, I worked three jobs. This took a toll on me physically. I couldn't sleep. I was extremely jittery. My elder sister made an appointment for me to see her primary-care doctor. He prescribed a sedative that helped me sleep and get some rest. After that, I just worked one job.

While growing up, I never had a complete medical examination and had no idea I had hypertension until I went for a physical for induction in the Armed Forces. I went for the physical about six weeks after I graduated college. After the physical, I was given a form and instructed to go to my doctor in two weeks to have my blood pressure checked and to give the doctor the form to complete and mail to the army induction office. When I had my pressure checked two weeks later, it was still high. As a result, I was put in class 1Y (not physically qualified for induction).

Also, while I was growing up, I never went to an eye doctor to have my eyes checked or to a dentist to have my teeth checked or cleaned. For years, I brushed my teeth with baking soda. I didn't use toothpaste until I was a teenager and had enough money to occasionally afford to buy a tube. I didn't go to an ophthalmologist, a medical doctor, or dentist on a regular basis until I graduated college and was gainfully employed. When I was twenty-four, I noticed my vision had gradually gotten blurred. I had my eyes checked by an ophthalmologist, and she found that I had congenital cataracts. Surgery wasn't warranted, and she wrote me a prescription for glasses.

In March of 1968, my father had a heart attack at home while watching television. He was rushed to the hospital, where he stayed for about one week. The attending cardiologist, who, incidentally, was our employer's doctor, told us the heart attack my father had was massive. To my knowledge, there was no surgical procedure done of any kind. When he was discharged, I don't remember him taking much medicine. He constantly complained of heartburn and took baking soda to get some relief.

When my father went home from the hospital, he was off work for six weeks. Fortunately, he was paid his salary of fifty dollars a week for six weeks. It was in the mid '60s that he got a raise from thirty dollars to fifty. If he wanted to continue to get paid, he had to return to work. We encouraged him to file for Social Security disability benefits, and he refused. There was nothing else we could do. I told him I would help him financially, but he returned to work anyway, knowing he wasn't physically able. I asked him why he went back to work so soon, and he told me his employer needed him back at work.

I'm sure, for whatever reason, he felt obligated to return to work. There is no question that he returned to work much sooner than he should have and probably shouldn't gone back to work at all. I am certain he was never encouraged by his employer to file for disability.

If he hadn't returned to work, his employer knew she wouldn't find anybody to do the work he did for what he was paid. I had no resentment toward his employer because he was an adult and he had his reasons for his decision. There was no doubt in my mind he returned to work because of his loyalty and he felt there was nothing else he could do. I can only imagine how helpless he must have felt over the years not being able to read or write and not having any specialized skills or training to seek other employment.

On July 1, 1968, while at work, my father had another heart attack and died. Fortunately, his employer helped with funeral expenses. When my father died, my mother was devastated. It was like she was lost without him. She would frequently tell us how much she missed him, and I could see the sorrow in her eyes and changes in her demeanor. She didn't have much of a social life. She went to church every Sunday and continued to spend a lot time working in the yard or in her vegetable garden. Occasionally, she and a friend would go fishing. Since she never learned to drive, she was totally dependent on somebody to take her places that weren't on the bus route.

My siblings (all of us lived out of town) and I agreed that we would take turns visiting on the weekends to keep her company, take her shopping, do yard work, and other things that needed to be done. These visits continued until we moved her from Montgomery to an assisted living facility in Birmingham, Alabama in 1995. My mother was very independent and refused to live with any of my siblings or me. When we moved her to the assisted living facility, I agreed to be responsible for ensuring her rent was paid on time, doctor's appointments were kept, and medication prescribed by the doctor was procured. My siblings and I decided that we should hire someone part time from 8:00 a.m. to 12:00 p.m. Monday through Friday to come in and cook for her and do some light household cleaning. After we found someone, I also agreed to be responsible for ensuring that this individual's performance was satisfactory and that she was paid on time. My younger brother, the doctor, provided on an ongoing basis the necessary additional financial assistance needed for our mother's care.

Since I didn't work very far from where my mother lived, I would check on her on my lunch break and sometimes take her something extra to eat for lunch or dinner. My elder brother, his wife, and our sister would also take her lunch or dinner periodically. I usually took her to the grocery store each week or went grocery shopping for her. My brother or I took her to church when she wanted to go. My wife and I, my brother and his wife, or our sister made sure she got breakfast, lunch, and dinner on the weekends. When my siblings or I went out of town to visit the other siblings or relatives, we always took her with us. We also took her to social functions and other activities in and outside Birmingham.

For years, my mother, my siblings and our children went fishing the Saturday the weekend of Labor Day. Usually, we caught about one hundred pounds of catfish, which we brought back to my house, cleaned it, and had a big fish fry. Invariably, there was enough fish for each family to take some home. We always got together with family on holidays. My mother strongly believed in having a close family and would frequently tell my siblings and me that we should always stick together and get together on happy occasions as often as possible.

My mother loved gardening. She had a garden at the assisted living facility where she lived. The assisted living facility had about an eighth of an acre of land it made available to tenants for gardening. She loved being outside and would frequently sit outside in the courtyard. She exercised religiously and walked at least one mile each day on the grounds of the assisted living facility (ALF) where she lived and on the parking lot of the hospital located adjacent to the ALF. She understood the benefits of exercise and being physically fit. Yet she continued to smoke. She was always diligent and conscientious about exercising on a regular basis and would exercise every day she was physically able to do so and the weather permitted. Before we moved her to Birmingham, she walked at least three miles a day in and around the neighborhood, visiting neighbors and periodically going to the grocery store.

In addition to gardening and walking, she looked forward to getting involved in things requiring physical activity, such as raking leaves, mowing grass, and trimming hedges. When she went walking in the neighborhood, she would often stop for a few minutes to chat with neighbors. She would chat with them about anything from her fishing trips, the Bible, to politics and current events. She was well informed. She always listened to news on the radio and watched it on television. She especially enjoyed religious sermons and gospel songs on both radio and television.

*****

God Will Take Care of You

Be not dismayed whatever betide, God will take of you.
Beneath his wings of love abide, God will take of you.
Through days of toil when heart doth
fail, God will take care of you.
When dangers fierce your path assail, God will take of you.
All you may need he will provide, God will take care of you.
Nothing you ask will be denied, God will take care of you.
No matter what may be the test, God will take care of you.
Lean weary upon his breast, God will take care of you.

Clothing/Attire

When my two older sisters were toddlers, my mother made them skirts and dresses out of flour sacks, especially those that had a floral design. In elementary school, I usually went to school barefooted until the weather turned cold. When I was in the third grade, it got cold before my parents could buy me a pair of shoes. The teachers took up a collection and bought me a pair of brown high-top leather shoes. I was somewhat embarrassed but thankful.

During the '40s and '50s, it was not unusual for country boys to wear overalls and one-piece long underwear. The long underwear had a slit in the lower front and a button-down flap in the lower rear to make it convenient to use the bathroom. Long underwear was quite beneficial in autumn and winter. I've owned my share. We also wore brogan shoes, a coarse work shoe reaching to the ankle. When my parents bought me clothes for school, they automatically bought me blue jeans and cotton shirts. The jeans and cotton shirts were bought because of the durability of the fabrics. Since these clothes had to last me for a while, they were bought a size too big to allow for growth. They basically had to last the entire school year. For Christmas, if I was lucky, I got a new pair of pants and maybe a shirt. New clothes and shoes especially during the school year were hard to come by. If there were any thrift stores or flea markets when I was growing up, we didn't know about them. Secondhand clothes would have been welcomed.

During the 1960s, fashion for men was not as revolutionary as it was for women, but there was a lot of change. Ties, belts, and lapels

115

got wider, collars got longer and wider, and a modified version of the bell bottom, called flared, became popular. The conservative men's suit took on some geometric design, along with the flare in the pants legs and wider lapels. Sports shirts were the norm for casual wear, with the polo style being the most popular. A lot of sports shirts were made of a material called Ban-Lon. Suit patterns grew bolder, as did color choices. Ties and shirts became more colorful as well.

Mod wasn't the only influence in men styles. The hippie movement brought about a philosophy that allowed for a greater choice in clothing. Vests were worn without the suit, sports jackets were worn with slacks, and suits with no tie. Although hippie clothing influenced mainstream style to a certain degree, it never caught on as an everyday fashion. By the end of the '60s, some fashions were here to stay. The flared dress slack would remain in style for another decade. Ties and lapels didn't skinny up for another twenty to twenty-five years.

When I was sixteen (1962), my favorite pair of shoes, even though they were two sizes too big, was a pair of black high-topped Stacey Adams shoes the doctor my dad chauffeured had owned. It was obvious they were expensive shoes, and when I shined them the toe of the shoes looked slick like glass. After the doctor's death, his daughter gave the shoes to my father, and he in turn gave them to me. They were in excellent condition. You could hardly tell that they had been worn. When I wore them, I had to stuff paper in the toe. I always made sure the bottom of my pant legs covered the top of the shoes to keep from being ridiculed because they were high-topped. On another occasion, the son of the folk we worked for gave my dad a pair of army boots that were in good condition. My dad also gave me the army boots. I asked myself, *What am I going to do with army boots?* Since I could use another pair of shoes, I decided to give them a good shine. They looked so good I wore them to school. Guess what? I got so many compliments before long a lot of the guys were buying army boots.

When I decided to dress up, I usually wore a brown sport coat, tan slacks, a white shirt, a brown tie, and brown socks and shoes. This was apparel I bought and had owned for a while and was the outfit I wore to church most of the time. During my senior year in high school, I joined the gentlemen's club and had to buy a navy-blue blazer. The uniform for the club was a navy-blue blazer, white shirt, gray trousers, royal-blue necktie and handkerchief with white polka dots, black belt, navy blue or black socks, and black shoes.

The gentlemen's club was a social club of twelfth-grade males who were academically motivated and consistently conducted themselves in a respectful and gentlemanly manner. If I'm not mistaken, several guys in the club who had the time occasionally provided after-school tutoring for about an hour two or three days a week. For Thanksgiving and Christmas, we collected food items for needy families; club-member families were excluded. In conjunction with the school, we collected money for the March of Dimes. Not having much money to buy clothes, I found that sport coats were more practical than a suit because I could change ties and slacks and have a different outfit.

In high school, I looked forward to the prom. The most popular and affordable attire for boys for the prom was a white jacket, white shirt, black bowtie, black cummerbund, black trousers, black shoes, and black socks. I started saving a little something early in the school year in preparation for the prom. I had to rent my outfit, buy a corsage for my date, put gas in the car, and have a little extra spending money for something to eat after the prom. I took two different girls to the prom my junior year. To one prom, as a courtesy, I took the daughter of a preacher. To my surprise, she just happened to have had two brothers at the prom. I was lucky. Haha! My date had strict parents and a 12:00 p.m. curfew. I didn't miss the curfew. The other girl I took to the prom was my girlfriend. Each prom was fun. Everybody was cheerful, excited, and ready to have fun dancing and enjoying the party atmosphere. The prom was a time when you were too busy having fun interacting and talking with classmates to think about anything other than just having fun. Some of the guys did a lot of girl watching and just enjoyed the party atmosphere.

Shopping for clothes and shoes was a challenge when you didn't have much money. I was a senior in high school and needed a pair of shoes to wear to a dance. So one Saturday after work, I went shopping. I was window-shopping this particular shoe store when I saw this beautiful pair of brown shoes on display. I had to have those shoes. I went inside. They had my size, and the price was right. The shoes were on sale for five dollars. I bought the shoes. The dance was the upcoming weekend, and I was looking forward to showing off my new shoes.

I wore the shoes to the dance. I was looking good. Unfortunately, it rained the night of the dance. When the dance was over it was pouring rain outside. My shoes got wet and my feet got wet. While I was driving home, something strange was happening to my shoes. My shoes didn't feel quite the same, and I felt air on my feet. When I got home and stepped out of the car, I looked down and saw that my shoes had lost their form and were separating at the sole. I couldn't believe what was happening. I was shocked and disappointed. I paid five dollars for the shoes, and five dollars back then wasn't easy to come by. Lesson learned, "If you buy a cheap pair of shoes, check the weather forecast before you wear them and never wear them on a rainy day."

It was awhile before I could afford to buy another pair of shoes. I had an old pair of brown shoes that had holes in the soles that I wore until I could buy another pair. I would put cardboard in the bottom of the shoes to cover the holes.

Transportation

From 1950 through 1968, my father owned several vehicles as follows: a green 1952 Chevrolet pickup truck, a light blue 1956 Ford Fairlane, a 1959 light-and-dark-blue Chevrolet Biscayne, and a 1963 light-blue Chevrolet Biscayne. When my elder brother went off to school, my father gave him the truck to drive. He drove the truck until he threw a rod in the engine while returning home from school one weekend. My father sold the truck and gave my brother the Ford to drive. My brother drove the Ford until he finished school, and then I drove it briefly for a while until the motor went bad. My father considered buying an engine for it, but a new engine cost more than the car was worth. Therefore, he junked it and, with the help of his employer, got the 1959 Biscayne.

I learned to drive when I was age twelve. My father taught me how to drive using a 1957 four-wheel-drive, straight-shift Jeep Willys. This vehicle was provided by my father's employer for him to drive when he checked on property located in Montgomery and Butler County. The car I drove when I got my license was the 1959 Chevrolet Biscayne. The lady for whom my dad worked bought the Biscayne for him. To pay for the car, my dad understood that five dollars a month would be held out of his pay. Clearly the car was an "el cheapo." The car was pre-owned, and I'm sure it didn't cost more than a few hundred dollars. The Biscayne had a six-cylinder engine and was the cheapest Chevrolet you could buy.

A 1959 six-cylinder Biscayne didn't have much horsepower. Here's an example. I liked a girl in Butler County who lived on the place where my father was the overseer. One Sunday afternoon, I decided to drive over to Butler County to visit her. The visit was nice. We had fun sitting in the swing on the porch, drinking Kool-Aid, checking out the barn, and just walking around in the yard. On the way back home, I got behind a car that was moving a little too slowly to my liking. We were traveling on a straight and level two-lane highway. I decided to pass. I signaled the car behind me and pulled out to pass. I mashed on the accelerator. The car didn't accelerate. I floored it; it barely picked up speed enough for me to drive side by side with the car I was trying to pass. In the meantime, the car behind me had moved up, closing the gap behind the car I was trying to pass. Looking ahead up the highway, I saw a car coming in my direction that I was meeting head-on. I didn't have enough speed to pass. I slowed down and signaled the driver behind me that I needed to move back over, and he let me in.

A few months later, I was involved in an accident and the car was totaled. I was driving east bound on a four-lane road on my way to work on Saturday morning when suddenly a car driven by this elderly man pulled out from an intersecting street and t-boned me on the passenger side. On impact, my vehicle was pushed slightly into the inside lane, where I was side-swiped on the driver side. Fortunately, no one was injured. Guess what? We got another six-cylinder Biscayne. This one was a sky-blue 1964 model that I drove until I graduated from college and moved from Montgomery. It was the family car, and I left it for my younger brother to drive.

Only a few people in the neighborhood owned cars. Interestingly, several of the neighbors who owned cars were mechanics. Several others who owned cars surprisingly had sufficient income to own a vehicle. People in the neighborhood, I'm sure, wondered for a while how could it be that my father could drive a new Jeep and we were as poor as we were. They were naturally curious, and we made it known that the Jeep my father drove wasn't his and explained why he kept it all the time. It was a tan eight- cylinder, four-wheel-drive Jeep Wagoneer. He kept the jeep 24/7 and was expected to drive anywhere at any time he was needed seven days a week.

Segregation and Discrimination

I was age nine when on December 1, 1955, a seamstress from Montgomery, Alabama, Mrs. Rosa Parks, after a long day's work, refused to give up her seat to a white man on a Montgomery City bus. It was a time in the South when separate facilities for blacks and whites were a reality, and if whites weren't satisfied with their facilities, the black man/woman was required to move or give way. Mrs. Parks was arrested, and after her arrest, a group of civic leaders called for a bus boycott on December 5, 1955, the day of Mrs. Parks trial. It was decided that the boycott would continue until (1) courteous treatment by the bus operators was guaranteed, (2) passengers were seated on a first-come, first-served basis, and (3) black bus operators were employed on predominantly black routes. The bus boycott ended on December 20, 1956, with a Supreme Court ruling.

The 1964 Civil Rights Act became law in July 1964. It was a landmark of legislative action to improve the quality of life for African Americans and other minority groups. The act did not resolve all problems of discrimination, but it opened the door for further progress. It lessened racial restrictions on the use of public facilities, provided more job opportunities, strengthened voting laws, and limited federal funding of discriminatory aid programs. Major features of the Act are as follows:

- Title I: Voting Rights - barred unequal application of voter registration requirements but did not abolish literacy tests sometimes used to disqualify African American and poor white voters.
- Title II: Public Accommodations - outlawed discrimination in hotels, motels, restaurants, theaters, and all other public accommodations engaged in interstate commerce; exempted private clubs without defining "private," thereby allowing a loophole.
- Title III: Desegregation of Public Facilities - permitted justice department suits to secure desegregation of certain public facilities.
- Title IV: Desegregation of Education - encouraged the desegregation of public schools and authorized the attorney general to file suits to force desegregation but did not authorize busing as a means to overcome segregation based on residence.
- Title V: Civil Rights Commission - addressed procedures for the commission, broadened its duties, and extended its life through January 1968.
- Title VI: Nondiscrimination in Federally Assisted Programs - authorized, but did not require, withdrawal of federal funds from programs which practiced discrimination.
- Title VII: Equal Employment Opportunity - outlawed discrimination in employment in any business exceeding twenty-five people and created an Equal Employment Opportunities Commission to review complaints, although it lacked meaningful enforcement powers.
- Title VIII: Registration and Voting Statistics - directed the Census Bureau to collect registration and voting statistics based on race, color, and national origin but provide that individuals could not be compelled to disclose such information.
- Title IX: Intervention and Removal of Cases - made reviewable in high federal courts the action of federal dis-

trict courts in remanding a civil rights case to state court and authorized the Attorney General to intervene in certain private suits.

- Title X: Community Relations Service - created the service to aid communities in resolving disputes relating to discriminatory practices based on race, color, and national origin.

I was age seventeen when the Civil Rights Act of 1964 was passed. When it became law, it not only included voting rights guarantees but also provided that a sixth grade education was a presumption of literacy for voting purposes. Nevertheless, blacks continued to experience difficulties throughout the South. Several civil rights organizations decided to focus attention on Alabama, one of the more intransigent states on the question of black voting.

Attempts to register blacks failed and a march from Selma to Montgomery was planned to dramatize the plight of Alabama's black citizens. The Selma to Montgomery march served as a stimulus for the Voting Rights Act (VRA) of 1965. The VRA contained provisions to assure blacks that devices previously employed to disenfranchise them would no longer serve this purpose. The new law authorized the attorney general to send federal examiners to register black voters when they concluded that local registrars weren't doing their job. It suspended all literacy tests and other devices in states and counties that used them and where less than 50 percent of the adults had voted in 1964.

On March 21, 1965, Dr. Martin Luther King and three thousand people began a five-day march from Selma to Montgomery. I was age eighteen when this event occurred. I heard on the radio detailed accounts of what took place. Unfortunately, due to my financial and economic situation and the possibility of jeopardizing my job and my father's job, I was not in a position to actively participate. But I could give my moral support. My parents, for fear of reprisal by my employer and the possibility of something terrible happening to me, were vehemently against my participation, especially after Jonathan Daniels and Viola Liuzzo were shot to death. A part-time white male deputy sheriff who fired the gun that killed Jonathan Daniels went to trial and was acquitted by an all-white jury. I could feel and sense the urgency and unrelenting impetus of the civil rights movement to bring about change—change to remove the social ills and disparities caused by racial segregation and discrimination.

During the '40s, '50s, and early '60s, blacks were expected to greet whites, regardless of age or gender, as "Yes, sir," "No, sir," "Yes, ma'am," or "No, ma'am." I witnessed my father doing this on countless occasions. I always thought to myself how demoralizing this must be for an adult black male to address a child in such a way. Apparently, my father and many other black adult males I observed didn't seem to have any visually detectable reservations about it. This is what was expected, and they accepted it. I think my father had been thoroughly indoctrinated and intimidated. He was overcome with fear and wouldn't have dared do otherwise. When you greeted or addressed a white adult, you were expected to say Mister, Missus, or Miss. This didn't bother me because this was what I was taught to say to adult blacks to show respect. When I was growing up during the '50s and '60s, I had very little contact with young whites. If I was in the presence of a young white, I stayed my distance to avoid having to say anything.

When it came to race relations, my parents did a good job of brainwashing me. They told me so many horror stories about how black males had been persecuted by whites, particularly in situations allegedly involving black males and white females. I was extremely careful what I did or said in a white female's presence. Psychologically, as a black male, I envisaged there was this boundary line that shouldn't be crossed. All of my young life, I heard of how black males were dealt with or would be dealt with if they crossed this line. The harsh consequences more often than not usually resulted from a black male being falsely accused of something. After desegregation, it was a few years into early adulthood that I became relatively comfortable in the presence of the white female.

Reflecting on how things were during segregation, it was automatic that if charges were brought against a black male for something that was considered criminal and you had to go to court, you would be facing an all-white jury. It goes without saying you would surely be found guilty. This line of thinking was confirmed in the Jeremiah Reeves case.

As reported by the local Montgomery newspaper, Jeremiah Reeves was originally charged with two counts of rape, two counts of assault with intent to rape, and one count of robbery. His first appeal to the US Supreme Court won a reversal of his first conviction. He was retried on the same charge and again convicted and given the death penalty. He lost his second appeal to the Supreme Court. A dramatic appeal for mercy during the clemency hearing produced a playback of a recorded confession and the insistent protest and emphatic declaration that he made the confession under pressure. Reeves told the governor's legal advisor that he was taken to the Kilby Prison execution chamber after his arrest and forced to sit in the bright-yellow electric chair while being questioned about a series of attacks on white women in the Montgomery area in 1952. He alleged that he was forced to admitting to the attacks on six women. On March 27, 1958, Jeremiah Reeves was electrocuted for the rape of a young Montgomery housewife. Around midnight, Reeves was brought to the execution chamber, and at 12:01 a.m., the first jolt of electricity stiffened his body. He continued to breathe and gasp slightly, and a second jolt at 12:06 a.m. was administered, and at 12:13 a.m., he was pronounced dead. It is my understanding that Reeves's accuser recanted her accusation several years later.

Generally, black males perceived the white female as double trouble. As a general rule, the black male stayed as far away from the white female as possible. I recall conversations I had with two of my cousins. They were much older than me and were involved in situations that demonstrated this fear. One cousin lived in Montgomery County and worked on a farm owned by whites. He was also a moonshiner. According to him, he made some of the best corn whiskey (also known as white lightning) in Montgomery County. The other cousin and his family were sharecroppers and lived on land owned by whites in Lowndes County.

The cousin who lived in Montgomery County told me that he went to work one day and was doing some yard work when the lady of the house called for him to come inside. Her husband was quite a distance from the house, plowing in the cornfield. When he went inside, she called him to the bedroom where she was lying totally naked—spread-eagle. He said he was terrified. He immediately left the house and went home. He said all he could think about was what could have happened if she for some reason had accused him of sexually assaulting her. The thought of what could have happened had he been accused of assault had such a psychological effect on him he decided to move from Montgomery County to Birmingham, Alabama, where two of his brothers lived. In the meantime, he had been busted twice for making moonshine. Shortly after moving to Birmingham, he got a job working in a coal mine.

The other cousin worked for a family that consisted of several girls. He said, for some reason, one girl in particular would always find her way to the cotton field where he was working. She would always sit or squat directly in front of him with her legs wide apart. He told me that she never had on panties and would just look at him and never said anything. After this happened a few times, he decided to tell his parents about the situation. They decided to send him out of state to live with an uncle. They told his boss that he had gotten a job out of state with his uncle installing ceramic tile.

In the South, during the '50s and early '60s, I remember it was common place for black males to be verbally degraded and in many instances physically beaten unjustifiably by whites, and nothing was done or could be done because blacks had no legal recourse. Most attacks were unwarranted and unjustified and were consistently squashed. Nothing could be proven because there was no tangible evidence, no witnesses or paper trail documenting the physical abuse and/or brutality that occurred.

I remember that racism was rampant during the '50s and '60s. One Saturday afternoon, I was age ten (1956), my older brother and I accompanied my father on a trip to Butler County, Alabama. While en route on Highway 31 South, one of the tires on the vehicle my father was driving went flat. Fortunately, we were near a roadside service station about twenty miles southwest of Montgomery. My father pulled in front of the service station. The jeep he was driving had a medical medallion attached to the front and rear tags (two tags were required). My father, having the appearance of a white man, was perceived to be white by the service-station attendant. When the tobacco-chewing, unshaven white male approached the vehicle, he noticed the medical medallion and immediately said, "What can I do for you, Doctor?" My father told him he had a flat tire, and the attendant replied, "Okay, Doc, I'll get on it right away." In the meantime, all I could think about was we were at a place that sold ice cream and I wanted some. I yelled to my father, "Daddy, buy me some ice cream." He signaled to me to be quiet. I had no clue why. The attendant finally repaired the tire. Getting impatient that I might not get any ice cream, I decided to yell quite loudly, "Daddy, don't forget the ice cream." The attendant heard what I said and, with a look of disgust, spit out a big splattering of tobacco juice and said rather loudly, "Goddammit, that's a goddamn nigger!" Needless to say, I didn't get any ice cream.

A few weeks after I got my driver's license, I took my mother to the doctor. When she signed in at the front desk, the receptionist smiled and asked her who was the handsome young man with her. My mother got really nervous and could hardly wait to see the doctor. This was in 1962. That was my first and last time taking her to that particular doctor. After that, when she had a doctor's appointment, she rode the city bus.

Present day, there is a lot of talk about racial profiling. This practice was quite common and noticeable during the '60s when I started driving. Numerous times, while driving in and around Montgomery or traveling outside the city, I was arbitrarily stopped by a policeman (especially in small rural towns) for a license check. There was no moving traffic violation and more often than not, I was referred to as "boy." Several of my relatives who lived up north told me that when they came South to visit and they stopped to get gas, they were usually referred to as "boy" as well and couldn't buy a Coca Cola because they were told, "Niggers don't drink Cokes. They're for white folk."

My senior year in college, I had the pleasure of knowing a local prominent white judge. I talked with him about some job possibilities as he had lots of contacts and knew a lot of important people in the right places. He said he would do some checking and get back with me. Within a few days, he contacted me and said he could get me a job at a local bank but there was one condition. He told me I would have to shave off my mustache. In the sixties, a mustache was considered a characteristic of black males, and to have a black male with a mustache working at a bank meeting and greeting white customers would have been bad for business and, most likely, offensive to the customers. I didn't pursue the job. My mustache was a natural part of my appearance, and I loved it. I think it made me look sexy, mature, and distinguished. I have it today.

In 1972, while traveling from Alabama to Mississippi on a liaison visit with an affiliate office of the federal agency for which I worked, I decided to stop for lunch in Mississippi at a roadside café. I entered the café and stood at the entrance for a few minutes, and no one came over to help me with seating. I spotted an empty table and went over and sat down. Although there were several waitresses, neither came over to take my order. After sitting there for a while visually surveying the café, I noticed that all of the customers and employees were white. As I continued to visually survey the facility, I noticed that two blacks on the outside had walked up to a window to place an order. All of a sudden, I realized that the café was still segregated, and I immediately left. I got in my car and drove about two miles down the highway and stopped at a restaurant that was in the motel of a well-known motel chain.

When I entered the restaurant, the receptionist took me to a table and gave me a menu. After looking over the menu, I got the waitress's attention and told her I was ready to order. Amazingly, they were out of everything I ordered. After ordering about four items on the menu, the waitress told me the only thing they had was fried chicken. She took my order and quickly returned and told me they were out of chicken also. I looked around, and I was the only black in the restaurant and everybody else was white and was eating. By now I was starving, and I decided to drive a little farther down the highway, where I stopped at the restaurant of another motel and, upon entering the restaurant, was immediately told they had a fire in the kitchen earlier and the restaurant was closed, although I saw several whites eating. I contacted the manager, a white male, at the office I was scheduled to visit and, with his assistance, was able to get something to eat.

The next day, I was scheduled to visit another office in a small town about thirty miles away. Therefore, I decided to go ahead and drive to the town and check in at the motel where I had reservations. When I arrived at the motel, I walked up to the front desk to check in and was greeted by an elderly white couple. I identified myself and told them why I was there. The elderly white lady, with a big smile, said, "They have a nigger manager at the office over there. He is really a nice nigger and is one of the nicest niggers I know." I was shocked speechless. I didn't say a word. I signed in and went directly to my room. For dinner, I ate snacks I got out of a vending machine. The next day, I visited the office I was scheduled to visit and immediately after my visit drove back to Alabama.

I couldn't believe what I had experienced the past three days. It was 1972, eight years after passage of the Civil Rights Act, and things should have changed by now. When I returned to the office, I was still in a state of shock. Was I so naïve to believe that things would have changed by then, or was it a simple matter of optimistically hoping things had?

During the mid through late '60s, my neighborhood had an outstanding sandlot baseball team. We consistently won most of our games. I don't think we ever had a losing season. Several guys on the team were really talented—two pitchers, a catcher, and a second baseman. These guys, in my opinion, could have played in the majors. Because of segregation and race discrimination, their talent went unrecognized. America missed another opportunity to see some talented black athletes play baseball, who could possibly have made the Baseball Hall of Fame.

Thanks to Dr. King and many others who participated in the civil rights movement and passage of the Civil Rights Act of 1964, many wonderful job opportunities were created for blacks, females, and other minorities. These job opportunities were in the private sector, including sports and education, and in city, county, state, and federal government.

*****

God's Tomorrow

God's tomorrow is a day of gladness
And its joys shall never fade
No more weeping, no more sense of sadness
No more foes to make afraid

God's tomorrow is a day of greeting
We shall see the savior's face;
And our longing hearts await the meeting
In that holy happy place.

God's tomorrow is a day of glory
We shall wear the crown of life
Sing through countless years love's old, old story
Free forever from all strife.

Social Life

There wasn't a YMCA or YWCA for blacks that was located within walking distance of the neighborhood. Therefore, we didn't have an opportunity to get involved in arts and crafts and athletic activities such as swimming and tennis. I learned to swim in a creek in Butler County. Several guys in the neighborhood learned to swim in a nearby fishpond.

On the north side of the house where I lived was a vacant lot. On the south side was a house with a family of seven—the parents, three girls, and two boys. One of the girls was my age. We were friends and, like other boys and girls our age, would occasionally play doctor-and-nurse, doctor-and-patient, nurse-and-patient, and other games. Doctor-and-nurse was a somewhat popular game with several girls in the neighborhood, and when I think about the incorrect terminology we must have used for medical devices and the male and female anatomy, the whole scenario was probably ridiculously funny or pathetic. Nonetheless, I must say it was nice growing up in a neighborhood where some of the girls were really friendly and adventurous and enjoyed having friendly fun.

When I was in the fourth grade, some classmates and I occasionally played spin-the-bottle on recess. There was this beautiful girl in the fifth grade who played the game with us. Wow! I had a crush on her. I was in love, but she didn't know it. Puppy love? One day, shortly after I fell in love, I didn't see her on recess anymore. I was heartbroken. *What happened?* I wondered. Upon inquiring about her, one of her former classmates told me that her family and she had moved across town. Regretfully, I never knew her full name. The next year, I was transferred to another school and never got the chance to get her full name from any of her former classmates. Whenever I was across town and I talked to someone I thought might know her, only giving them her first name, I would ask if they knew anyone by that name. Nobody I asked knew her. I always wondered what happened to her.

When thinking about her a few years later, it occurred to me that several students attending the school at the time were "military brats." One or both parents may have been in the Air Force and were stationed at Maxwell Air Force Base. Rather than moving across town, her parents were probably reassigned to another base, and they moved out of state or out of the country. She probably didn't notice me and don't know I ever existed.

In the ninth grade, I met a girl to whom I was highly attracted. She attended a private school. She was a very attractive, petite, light-brown-skinned girl with black wavy hair. Her older brother was likewise attracted to my older sister. Our families developed a close friendship that has continued.

In the tenth grade, I met a girl who attended the same school I attended. She was light-brown skinned also, had a beautiful smile, and had long, wavy hair that hung well below her shoulders. I found her to be very materialistic and didn't have the social and spiritual maturity of the girl who attended private school. For Valentine's Day, I decided to give the girl at my school a box of chocolate-covered cherries. An organization at the school was selling the candy for a fund raiser. The cherries cost a $1.00 or $1.50. This was what I could afford. I was doing something nice. She didn't take the cherries; she was offended. I too was offended because she refused them. Times were hard, and that was what I could afford. We remained on speaking terms, and I concluded that she wasn't familiar with the saying "It's the thought that counts." I gave the other girl a Valentines card, which she liked and appreciated. I explained to her that I couldn't afford to buy her any chocolate Valentine's candy. My family and I ate the cherries.

Dating was tough. Mothers and grandmothers alike put the fear of God in girls when it came to dating. It was hard to get a good passionate kiss. You could easily scare a girl off if you were too aggressive when you went out on a date. This happened to me. I scared off a girl that I really liked. The incidence of teenage pregnancy among high school girls during the late '50s and early '60s was relatively low. The last thing a girl's family needed was another mouth to feed and the embarrassment of the daughter having a child out of wedlock and dropping out of school. Times were hard in many respects, and money wasn't easy to get. There were some girls, however, who were promiscuous (probably out of curiosity). These girls usually got a bad reputation, and if you were smart, you kept your distance in more ways than one.

Generally, girls weren't very forward in starting relationships because it was considered not ladylike. Usually, if a girl liked you, she or her friend in a subtle way would let you know. If you were interested, it was up to you to initiate contact or make the first move. If I were young, single, and dating today, I would be elated if a girl approached me to let me know she is interested. Personally, I see nothing wrong with a female being forward, assertive, and maybe even slightly aggressive in getting the attention of someone in whom she is interested. For me, this would certainly make dating a lot easier. If I didn't want to date the female who approached me, I would simply say, "I'm sorry but I'm already in a relationship." This would be a suave and diplomatic way of saying "I'm not interested."

In today's climate, the old-school way of thinking that it's not ladylike for the female to approach the male is passé or outmoded. Also, in approaching someone to let the person know you're interested, I prefer the direct approach, such as "Hello, my name is Nathan, and I would like to get to know you. This is my phone number, and I'm looking forward to hearing from you." If she takes the number and calls—or if she doesn't, I haven't lost anything. You win some, and you lose some.

I dated several girls in high school. However, I had two steady girlfriends—one in the eleventh grade through the first half of the twelfth grade, and one during the second half of the twelfth grade, which lasted through the first semester of my freshman year of college. During my sophomore year in college, I dated a young lady who was a senior at the college I attended. When I first met her, I was in the library studying. I just happened to look up, and there was this beautiful young lady with a red dress on, a knockout physique, walking past the room where I was studying. I couldn't resist the attraction. I immediately went outside and introduced myself. I emphatically told her she was the most beautiful girl I had ever seen and I would be devastated if she didn't give me her phone number. She gave me her number and told me where she lived. We talked on the phone several times and the romance began. We had a good relationship up until the month she graduated. She did something that caused me to question her commitment to the relationship that I couldn't accept, and we parted ways. Apparently, I was more committed to the relationship than she. She moved out of the city, and I didn't talk with her again for about twenty-five years. My junior year, I started dating a girl who was also a junior. This relationship lasted several years.

There was not a lot to do on a date. On the west side of town, which is where I lived, there was a popular sandwich shop where teens would hang out on the weekends after football and basketball games. We didn't have skating rinks, bowling alleys, or amusement parks. The main attraction for black teens going out on a date was the movies. There were three indoor movie theatres and one drive-in for blacks. There was also a drive-in for whites near the neighborhood where I lived that one of my cousins and some of her friends frequented. My cousin was very light skinned and had red hair. When she needed to, she easily passed for white. Also, she had two first cousins who easily passed for white who would accompany her to the drive-in. When she, her cousins, and/or her friends went to the all-white drive-in, the ones who weren't light enough would hide underneath a blanket on the backseat until they gained entry. They would park in the rear to keep from attracting attention.

If you didn't go to the movies, you could always take your date to a high school sports event, to church, or to a sandlot baseball game on Saturday or Sunday afternoon. Going clubbing where alcoholic beverages supposedly weren't served to teens attracted some teenagers. I went to a club a few times to attend birthday parties. Clubbing never appealed to me. I didn't smoke, but some of the teens did. When I was age fourteen, I secretly smoked several of my mother's cigarettes. I didn't like the bad taste the smoke left in my mouth. Consequently, I never had a desire to smoke. At the clubs, some of the teens probably drank beer and maybe alcohol.

As far as my consumption of alcohol goes, I only drank one martini when I served martinis at social gatherings where I worked. One martini wasn't intoxicating, and one was all I wanted. I guess the vermouth I mixed with the gin and vodka lessened the effect of the alcohol. When I was a teenager, other than the martini where I worked, I never drank any other alcohol or had a desire for it. When I became an adult, I experimented with tasting different types of wine, champagne, and liquor such as scotch, bourbon, brandy, gin, vodka, and rum. I never saw the benefit of drinking alcohol because after a couple of drinks, depending on the strength of the alcohol, I'm somewhat in a stupor. I don't like feeling lethargic or being in a daze.

I enjoyed dancing but never went to a club for that purpose. To me, clubs tended to attract the bad element and wasn't a good place to hang out. When I was in the twelfth grade, a close friend of mine went to a neighborhood club one night and talked to a girl he knew had been flirting with him. He didn't know she had a jealous boyfriend who had gone outside to his car. When the boyfriend returned, he and my friend had an altercation. The girl's boyfriend had a sawed-off shotgun that he pulled on my friend. My friend grabbed the barrel as the gun fired. He lost his right hand and most of his lower right arm. My friend was hospitalized for a couple of weeks.

After hospitalization, my friend went through occupational therapy. He didn't let his physical impairment stop him from finishing high school. He also graduated from college obtaining a bachelor's degree and a masters degree. He taught high school several years and was an assistant principal when he retired. We both enjoyed fishing. Although he had a physical impairment, he was determined to continue to bass and crappie fish. He learned to use his right arm in such a way that he could fish as well as anybody with two hands and arms. Sadly, he is no longer with us. He had kidney failure and went on dialysis for about ten years. Several years ago, he had a heart attack and died.

My family never went anywhere for fun, relaxation, and recreation. In other words, we never took a vacation. We didn't know what a vacation was. We were always at home year in to year out. My father worked seven days a week (holidays included) January 1 through December 31. The only times we did something together as a family was on a weekend when we went to church, went to visit relatives that lived nearby, or when we went to a funeral or a wedding.

When my siblings and I were growing up, my elder and middle sisters were the only ones of us to travel outside the state of Alabama. My maternal grandmother took them on a trip with her on separate occasions via train to Chicago, Illinois, and Cincinnati, Ohio. A round-trip coach ticket to Chicago and Cincinnati via train didn't cost very much and was something my grandmother could afford because she and two of her sisters lived together in a house that was owned by my mother's youngest sister's husband. She and her sisters shared household expenses, and as a result, each of them was able to save some money. My mother's youngest sister's husband was a carpenter by trade and built the house in which my grandmother and her sisters lived. He built several houses in the neighborhood where he and my aunt lived and rented them to neighbors. He was quite knowledgeable and skillful in different facets of home building involving electrical wiring, heating and cooling, and plumbing. He was also a skilled mechanic

I don't remember ever having a birthday party where friends along with family were invited. Birthdays were usually celebrated with immediate family only. I never received a gift on my birthday that had much value (a handkerchief or a cheap pair of socks). When we celebrated birthdays, a homemade cake, lemonade, and possibly homemade ice cream were served. There was always at least one candle on your birthday cake. I blew out a lot of candles and made a lot of wishes that never materialized. However, I was invariably hopeful that eventually things would get better.

*****

Somebody Cares

Somebody knows when your heart aches,
And everything seems to go wrong;
Somebody knows when the shadows
Need chasing away with song;

Somebody knows when you are lonely,
Tired, discouraged, and blue;
Somebody wants you to know him,
And know that he dearly loves you.

Somebody knows when you are tempted,
And your mind grows dizzy and dim;
Somebody cares when you are weakest,
And fartherest away from him.

Somebody grieves when you are fallen,
You are not lost from his sight;
Somebody waits for your coming,
And he'll drive the gloom from your night.

Somebody loves you when you are weary,
Somebody loves you when you are strong;
Always waiting to help you,
He watches you one of the throng;

Needing his friendship so holy,
Needing his watch-care so true;
His name? We call his name Jesus;
He loves everyone, he loves you.

Education

Only a few kids in the neighborhood (girls and boys) in my age group attended high school and graduated. I enjoyed school and looked forward to going each day. I was eager to learn something new. It was exciting to take different subjects and learn about so many different things. I also enjoyed the extracurricular facet of school. In junior and senior high, I played in the marching and concert bands.

It was by accident that I became interested in playing a musical instrument. One Saturday afternoon, my dad and I went to visit my uncle in Lowndesboro to go coon hunting. When my uncle went in the closet to get his hunting clothes, I noticed a silver trombone on the top shelf. I asked him about it, and he told me he played in the band when he was in the army. I asked him if he had any plans to do anything with it. He said he didn't and offered it to me. That's when I became seriously interested in music. I was in the eighth grade. I took a class in music and learned to play the trombone well enough to join the marching and concert bands. I was first trombone in both bands until I graduated. The concert band usually played at assembly programs, graduation, and other functions. I especially enjoyed playing in the marching band. We went on several out-of-town trips (nowhere very far) each year for football games and band competition. Therefore, I got to see different places and meet new people. I went places I never would have gone (e.g., Tuskegee, Sylacauga, Anniston, and Tuscaloosa, Alabama) had I not played in the band. Another benefit of playing in the band was that we ate free. I welcomed a free meal.

I didn't play in the band in college because I had to work. Knowing that I had to work, I didn't apply for a music scholarship. Playing in the band would have consumed too much of my time. Therefore, I wouldn't have had any money for gas, food, and entertainment. If I didn't work, I didn't have any spending money. There was no one I could go to for financial assistance.

To my knowledge, I'm the only one in my age group in the neighborhood to attend college and graduate. In view of the stressed living conditions I had to deal with, I'm blessed I did well enough academically to finish high school. Upon graduating from high school, I wasn't sure what I was going to do. While I was growing up, I always said I wanted to be a bricklayer. Shortly after finishing high school though, I had a change of heart. I knew then I wanted to attend college, but I just couldn't see how I could afford it. My family was poor, and I didn't have anybody to help me financially. Therefore, it was very easy for me to be discouraged and disheartened, but I didn't give up. Somehow, I knew I would find a way to go to college. The Lord sent me the answer.

My oldest sister and I were chatting one day, and the issue of college came up. She reminded me that I did well academically in high school (I graduated no. 18 in a graduating class of 251) and that I should consider going to college. She said I was smart and had the aptitude and intellectual ability. Her words inspired me. Also I remembered what my mother would sometimes say, "Where there is a will there is a way." I applied for admission to Alabama State University (formerly Alabama State College) and was accepted. Once I was accepted, I had to devise a plan to be financially able to buy books and school supplies and pay tuition. So I decided that I would work during the summer and save all my money. Fortunately, I was able to save enough to pay tuition and buy all my books and school supplies the first semester. However, I quickly realized that I had to continue to work while I was in school. As soon as my last class was over each day, I immediately went to work. The Higher Education Act of 1965 (Pell Grant) was passed by Congress and signed into law on November 8, 1965. Not having access to the necessary forms of news media or communiqué publicizing the act, I never knew it existed while I was in school, and no one I came in contact with at school ever mentioned it.

I worked off campus. There were many days I wanted to stay on campus for a while to socialize with classmates and spend time at the library reading and studying. The thing I hated most about having to work six and sometimes seven days a week was not having a chance to study as much as I desired. As a result, I found myself cramming for test after test after test. Having to do that, I knew I wasn't performing at the level of my potential. I have always believed in giving 100 percent. When I think about college to this day, it bothers me psychologically knowing that I wasn't able to perform at the level of my capability. Although I had a high scholastic average (graduating in the top 10 percent of my class), I'm sure it would have been much higher had I been able to devote more time to studying.

Even though I worked a lot, I enjoyed college. To me, your college days, if you are fortunate enough to attend college, are probably the best days of your young adult life. You have this unique opportunity to meet many interesting people with varied backgrounds, interests, and life experiences that are concentrated in a relatively small locale. When you attend college, it's like you instantly become an adult. You become more psychologically and emotionally mature and independent. You make your own decisions. The whole college experience can be quite enriching and rewarding, especially when you are focused and cognizant of why you are there in the first place.

Had I been able to spend more time on campus, I would have been in an excellent position to take advantage of valuable academic and nonacademic resources that were available. Another advantage of spending more time on campus is that it would have increased my popularity that became a factor when I ran for president of the student government association (SGA). Since I spent very little time on campus I wasn't widely known by the student body at large. This was to my disadvantage. In spite of my lack of popularity though, I came in a close second out of the three candidates, only ten votes shy of winning. I'm sure the speech I gave when I was campaigning helped me do as well as I did. My speech focused on the need to work more closely with the administration in apprising them of student body concerns and providing ideas about some things that could be done to improve the curriculum, campus grounds and building facilities, cultural, and enrichment activities in arts (dance and theatre). I emphasized the importance of the administration getting input from the SGA in developing initiatives to attract more students and a more diversified faculty. The primary theme of my speech was to improve communications between the administration and the student body and to insure that student concerns were expeditiously addressed.

In spite of devoting much of my time to work, I made the dean's list most semesters. I graduated with honors finishing in the top 10 percent of my class. While matriculating at Alabama State, I was inducted into the Sigma Rho Sigma Honor Society and Who's Who among Students in American Universities and Colleges and elected president of my fraternity my senior year. Because of my scholastic standing and achievements, I was offered a fellowship in history at Carnegie Mellon University (CMU) in Pittsburgh, Pennsylvania. In the meantime, I participated in job interviews with an agency of the federal government and International Paper company. I was quite pleasantly surprised and intrigued by the fellowship offer from CMU. I really wanted to accept the fellowship. I knew it would have been a tremendous opportunity to further my education and give me a chance to explore new educational and employment possibilities. However, the job offer with the federal government was too attractive to turn down. I was looking forward to having a decent income. The pay for the job I was offered was too lucrative not to accept. I accepted the job and had a long, enjoyable career with the government.

With the encouragement of our parents, my siblings and I were determined to get an education beyond high school. Our parents instilled in us the value of an education. Their expectation in this regard was quite high. They believed it was imperative that we learn a skill, a trade, or get a college education.

My elder brother is a tailor and owns and operates a tailoring business. He is semiretired. My elder sister earned an associate degree in secretary science. She is retired. My middle sister who is also retired became a seamstress and did work for several clothiers while self-employed. It is interesting that she and our brother the tailor never became partners. My sister is quick to tell you without hesitation that they couldn't work together because he is too much of a perfectionist and too impatient. Although she did excellent work, she decided that it would not be at a pace to his liking, as he was more production oriented. My youngest sister is a registered nurse and is presently retired.

My youngest brother is a practicing ophthalmologist. He earned a bachelor of arts degree at Alabama State University. After completing coursework toward a master's degree at Alabama State, he decided to attend medical school and earned a degree in medicine at the University of Iowa School of Medicine. Upon graduating, he did his internship at a hospital in Kalamazoo, Michigan. He did his residency at Massachusetts Eye and Ear Infirmary at Harvard University's Medical School in Boston, Massachusetts. Subsequently, he completed a fellowship at Emory University in Atlanta, Georgia, specializing in glaucoma. He owns the building where he practices and has a staff of five. He has an eyeglass business on site, where he sells a large array of frames for males and females. He employs an optician who handles all the logistics involving frame selection, fitting, and lens preparation and installation.

The same as our parents, my siblings and I continually encouraged our children when they were in school to study hard, make good grades, and get a good education. As parents, we worked hard to provide them with everything they needed to be successful in their academic and nonacademic or extracurricular pursuits. We worked hard at trying to be good role models and instill in them values such as self-respect, pride, honesty, and integrity. We stressed the importance of being selective in choosing friends, striving for excellence, and always doing their best.

All of my nieces and nephews are living except my oldest sister's daughter, who was killed in an automobile accident at age sixteen and my oldest brother's middle son who died of cancer in his late forties. My elder brother has three sons and two daughters, my elder sister has one son, my middle sister has two sons, my youngest sister has a son and a daughter, and my youngest brother has two sons. I have three sons and two daughters. All of my children, my nieces, and my nephews graduated high school and either learned a trade, earned an associate, a bachelor's, or master's degree. Three of my nephews are self-employed.

My siblings and I, except the youngest brother, have grandchildren. My elder brother has three boys and six girls, my elder sister has two boys, my middle sister has three boys, my youngest sister has two boys and two girls, and I have two boys and six girls.

Me at 19, a sophomore in college

Life After College

I met my wife a few years after I moved to Birmingham. She was a teller at the bank where I cashed my paychecks. When I first saw her, I found her to be very attractive. She had this pretty face and curvaceous figure that I admired more and more each time I saw her. She really got my attention. I couldn't stop thinking about her. When I spoke with her, she was always pleasant and greeted me with a beautiful smile. Now I was thinking she was attracted to me as much as I was to her. When I went to the bank, which was quite often, I would always engage her in a brief conversation.

After I had known her for about a month, I decided I was going to ask her out on a date, but it didn't happen the way I had planned. One Monday morning, after I had gone fishing over the weekend, I had to go to the bank to transact some business. I always went to her window, and as usual, I engaged her in a conversation. I told her about my fishing trip and that I caught lots of fish. Her coworker overheard the conversation and asked me if I had anybody to cook the fish. I said I didn't, and the coworker immediately told me that the young lady (my future wife) with whom I was talking would be glad to cook it for me. It put her on the spot, and she couldn't say no when I asked her if she would cook it. She said she would, and that was exactly what I wanted to hear. I cleaned the fish as soon as I got home from work and took it to her house for her to keep it in the refrigerator. I was excited.

The following Saturday, she fried the fish and invited me to her house for dinner. With the fish, she served baked potatoes, corn on the cob, tossed salad, and ice tea. The meal was delicious. This was one of several meals she prepared for me, and I concluded she was a good cook. We dated for six months, and I proposed to her. She accepted. Three months later, we got married. My wife had two things in common with me that really got my attention when we were dating—she grew up in church and worked her way through college.

When my wife and I got married, we decided we would wait three months before we started a family. We have three children, two sons and a daughter. We both were heavily involved in their upbringing. We took them to church on Sundays and did a lot of other things together as a family. Also, we spent a lot of time doing things with them that involved school and after-school extracurricular activities. We were active in the PTA, and one of us usually held office as president or another position in the PTA organization. My wife and I always encouraged our children to do their best, conduct themselves in a respectful manner, and stay out of trouble. We stressed the importance of doing well academically and choosing the right kind of friends. All three of them participated in little league, middle school, and high school sports. They each graduated with honors and received academic scholarships to college.

I had a successful career with the federal government. I started my career as a GS-5 technical employee and advanced to a temporary GS-14 management position before I retired. In June 1968, I entered federal employment in a career-ladder position (GS5/7/8). In January 1973, I was promoted to a GS-9 technical position. Eight months later, I was selected for the Management Intern Program (a two-year management-training program). This position was a career ladder GS 9/11/12 position. Upon completion of the program, I worked in a GS-12 staff position and a managerial position. In 1981, I was promoted to a GS-13 management position and, twelve years later, to a temporary GS-14 management position in 1993. At the agency where I worked, the turnover rate in management level positions was extremely low. Therefore, there was very little room for advancement unless you were mobile and willing to relocate. For health reasons and to take advantage of a federal workforce restructuring incentives program, I retired in January 1995. Throughout my career with the government, I received monetary awards based on excellent or outstanding performance.

When I retired, I was age forty-eight and had three children (ages nine, thirteen, and sixteen) in school. Therefore, I decided I needed to find a job to supplement my retirement annuity. I wanted a job that didn't involve a lot of stress and allowed me to wear casual clothes. Since I had a college degree and was qualified to teach, I thought about applying for a teaching position but quickly decided that the stress level would be too high.

As fate would have it, a few months after I retired, I went on a field trip with my daughter. While on the field trip, I decided to talk to the school-bus driver about hours of work, pay, and qualification requirements for the bus-driver position. Without hesitation, the driver provided me with the information I needed. To qualify for the school-bus-driver position, she told me I needed to get a class B (passenger endorsement) commercial driver's license (CDL). I applied for the job, got my CDL, and was hired. The pay was acceptable, and the hours of work, 6:00 a.m. to 8:30 a.m. and 2:00 p.m. to 4:30 p.m., Monday through Friday, were perfect. This work schedule allowed me all the time I needed to visit with my mother during the day, take her to the doctor, take her shopping, and help her with her gardening. It also allowed me to occasionally have lunch with my children at school and to talk with their teachers.

Before I retired from driving the bus, I drove for three separate school systems. In each system, I was fortunate to have had an opportunity to transport students who were respectful and generally well behaved. In addition to driving the bus at one of the schools where I worked, I also worked as a janitor and learned a lot about the equipment used in stripping and buffing floors.

I have always been willing and excited about learning to do something new and different. New experiences often create entrepreneurial opportunities. Learning about new things and learning to do new things provide you an opportunity to grow intellectually and may sometimes result in one reaching new economic and financial horizons.

Words Of Wisdom

During the sixty-nine years I have lived, I've learned a lot and can offer some words of wisdom. Therefore, I have developed the following words of wisdom based on things I experienced in dealing with people in the workplace and in social settings in general. The philosophical concepts I have developed, with which you may or may not agree, are food for thought and should be a good tool to use in day-to-day living. Since they worked well for me, I shared many of them with my children and decided to include them in this transcript to share with you. Hopefully, there is something under this chapter that will be helpful to you in making an important decision or at least give you something to think about while facing life's many challenges.

- Think before you act and always think about the consequences of your actions.
- When you meet someone you are attracted to, make sure that person shows genuine interest in you before you get too involved. Otherwise, you may be setting yourself up for heartbreak and disappointment.
- Get to know a person at a distance before you get too emotionally attached. Determine if you have enough in common before you start a serious relationship.
- Be prepared to accept a person the way he or she is in terms of ideology, values, personality, and religious beliefs. What you see is usually what you get.

- Love yourself and feel good about yourself. Remember you are God's creation and He doesn't make mistakes.
- Don't compromise your ethical and moral standards just to have someone like you. Look for someone who is willing to accept you the way you are.
- Sometimes it's good to give, but know where to draw the line. It is true that some people will take advantage of you because they take kindness for weakness.
- If someone does something nice for you, you should at some point reciprocate as necessary or do something nice for someone else. Don't always be on the receiving end.
- Think before you repeat what you hear about someone. Don't become a gossipmonger. There are always three sides to every story.
- When you receive a blessing, look for ways to give a blessing.
- Judge not. No one is perfect.
- Be trustworthy and a person of integrity. Do what you say you will do and say what you mean.
- Always strive to do the right thing to the extent that based on your knowledge and experiences you know what the right thing is.
- A serious relationship should be based on love, respect, honesty, friendship, and trust.
- When you are in a serious relationship or marriage, you should be considerate of your partner's needs and concerns. They should not be ignored. Be caring, nurturing, and reassuring. Communication is important.
- In marriage, be careful of outside friendships especially male/female. The average man or woman is possessive and wants his or her partner's undivided attention.
- If someone with whom you are not interested in being friends approaches you, be direct in what you say and how you say it. Leave no room for misinterpretation and misunderstanding.
- In a serious relationship, determine those things that are most important to you (realistically within reason) and

don't settle for less than what you want. A relationship can be long term, and you don't want to have any regrets.

- If a person with whom you are contemplating a relationship has a really annoying or irritating idiosyncrasy, you might want to look further.

- Before you make an important decision and you feel you need some advice, don't hesitate to talk with someone you trust and respect.

- Set goals and develop a plan. There may be obstacles along the way, but you make adjustments and continue to press forward.

- Life is precious. Enjoy it as much as you can each day. Have a positive attitude and outlook on life. There is just as much beauty in rain as there is in sunshine.

- Don't let a person with a negative attitude hold you back or drag you down. If necessary, get new friends who are positive thinkers and move on.

- Don't overextend yourself financially. Be patient. In time, you will get the things you want. You can live and be happy with less than you think.

- Pursue a career or profession in something you believe you will enjoy. You can spend a lot of time on the job. It may not be as lucrative as you would like, but you will be happy doing what you do.

- Don't let someone else decide a career for you. It's your life. You decide. Pursue your own dreams.

- Don't live in the past. There's nothing you can do to change it. We all have made mistakes. Live in the present, stay focused, and look forward to the future. God has something good in store for you.

- Save! Plan for the future. Put some money aside for emergencies and unexpected expenses.

- Family is important. Spend quality time with family and do fun things with them as often as possible.

*****

Whenever I am worried, stressed, troubled, somewhat anxious, or just want to feel at ease, I pray and then I slowly read or recite Psalm 23. The words in Psalm 23, when you slowly read or recite them, have a very calming, relaxing, and quieting effect. Take a few minutes and slowly read Psalm 23.

> The Lord is my shepherd; I shall not want.
>
> He maketh me to lie down in green pastures: he leadeth me beside the still waters.
>
> He restoreth my soul: he leadeth me in the paths of righteousness for his name's sake.
>
> Yea, though I walk through the valley of the shadow of death, I will fear no evil: for thou art with me; thy rod and thy staff they comfort me.
>
> Thou preparest a table before me in the presence of mine enemies: thou anointest my head with oil; my cup runneth over.
>
> Surely goodness and mercy shall follow me all the days of my life: and I will dwell in the house of the Lord for ever.

Now that you have read Psalm 23, hopefully you feel relaxed and at ease. Sometimes, to feel the full effect of the words, you have to read or recite it more than once. Read or recite it as many times as you need to. May God bless you with good health, peace of mind, prosperity, and happiness. And as you continue on life's journey, may He lead and guide you and keep His arms of protection around you.

Some Things To
Think About

We are all God's children. He loves each of us equally and unconditionally. So let each of us be more Godlike and resolve to work toward
being devoid of hypocrisy and work toward loving one another
unconditionally. Also, let each of us resolve to treat one another with
civility and mutual respect.

God wants each of us to enjoy a life of prosperity. Young people, I implore you to prepare yourself to achieve prosperity. Also,
I urge you to resolve to grow intellectually and to excel academically. You have to get an education. If you need to do extra work
to complement classroom instruction, self-help educational material
is available to you in your school library. Also, the public library
houses a vast array of educational material and equipment for you
to use free of charge. Therefore, everyone, whether you are a teenager or an adult, has an opportunity to increase one's knowledge in
various subject-matter areas from an educational standpoint. Each
library contains state-of-the-art educational material and is an excellent place for self-improvement. The library is equipped with the
Internet and desktop computers that are user-friendly. Also available are computer hardware and software containing information on
almost anything you would like to know more about or learn about.
In today's technologically advanced society, it would be advantageous
for the younger generation, within the framework of the law, to learn
as much as they can, as fast as they can, in specific areas of interest

to equip themselves with the knowledge, training, skills, and abilities they need to earn a good living, allowing them to achieve and maintain a good quality of life.

The necessity of young people getting a good education cannot be overemphasized. Parents of young children should take more responsibility to ensure that their children get at least a high school diploma. This will allow them an opportunity to seriously compete for jobs and increase their chances for employment. With such a wealth of information available via various computer software, none of us should operate in a realm of ignorance or a lack of preparedness. Young and not-so-young adults, as often as you can, should encourage youths to take advantage of available educational and employment opportunities (scholarships, educational grants, internships, co-ops, and other available financial-assistance programs). Young blacks should be reminded continuously that many individuals made great sacrifices to open doors of opportunity for them and other minorities so they could have a chance to climb the ladder of success and live a good life.

Women, without a doubt, should receive equal pay for equal work without gender being a consideration. Taking into account the sex of an individual in determining pay in jobs that both males and females can do should not be accepted and tolerated, and anytime someone becomes aware of this discriminatory occurrence it should be publicized. Historically, women in certain jobs have consistently been paid less than men for the same or similar work. Women are just as qualified and capable as men and should be paid at the same rate of pay as their male counterpart for the same or comparable work.

It is imperative that we as parents, grandparents, friends, and neighbors get involved (individually and collectively as necessary) in the lives of young blacks and others, especially those in single parent homes, to try and keep them on track scholastically. Single moms, in an ongoing friendly and diplomatic manner, should encourage their children's absentee fathers to get involved in their children's lives, showing them love, providing moral support and encouragement, and being good role models.

It seems that spirituality doesn't exist in many homes as it once did. It needs to be restored. We have to somehow get all teenagers attention regarding the serious consequences of illegal drugs and unprotected sex and try and discourage them from having children out of wedlock. We have to somehow instill in them the value of making good choices and getting a good education. They need to understand the urgency of making education a priority. Being poor, uneducated, unskilled, and having no specialized training to get a good job is pure torment. I know. I have seen it. We also have to somehow instill in all black youths the importance of self-worth and being proud African Americans unwilling to perpetuate ignorance and poverty. I am quite aware that at times there may be situations and extenuating circumstances adversely impacting one's ability to achieve one's goals, but you must be resilient and never give up. Black youths cannot allow themselves to be unprogressive. They have to press forward. The My Brother's Keeper initiative instituted by President Obama is a good example of something positive being done to exhort, support, and encourage young blacks to do what they need to do to achieve success.

Socioeconomically, many things obviously are a lot better today for blacks and other minorities including women. However, we still have a long way to go. There are still barriers and obstacles that we have to overcome. Unfortunately, we still have to deal with racial profiling, racial prejudice, and subtle segregation. At this point, I have to paraphrase a familiar cliché that I have already used because it is undoubtedly apropos: "The more things change, the more they remain the same." For example, demographics (due to white flight) are such that a lot of inner-city schools' student enrollment in many cities are all or almost all minority (black or black-other). This is tantamount to racial segregation, but to a lesser degree, as we knew it a few decades ago. The CRA mandated that public schools should be integrated.

The US is perceived as a land of opportunity and a melting pot of many individuals of different cultures and nationalities. Melting pot is a place where racial amalgamation and social and cultural assimilation are going on. When cultures are melted together, they should blend and come together and work in harmony and with compassion, compatibleness, and concern for one another. We are not there yet. It appears that skin color continues to come into play and is a factor in a negative way in the results of decisions that are made that impact the lives of blacks and other minorities in the three major facets of life (political, economic, and social). Therefore, blacks, in particular, cannot become lax and apathetic allowing things to move backward toward status quo ante. Get off your rear end and vote. Ferguson, Missouri, the 2014 mid-term elections, and the 2016 presidential primaries should be a wakeup call.

Having read "Some Things to Think About," ask yourself this question: what can I do in a genuinely positive and sincere way to help things change socially, economically, or politically so that everyone has an equal opportunity to be successful in life and is truly accepted and integrated into the melting pot regardless of race, color, religion or sexual preference?

As we continue our quest for equal opportunity for all Americans, let us keep God at the center of our lives and don't forget to pray.

"I can do all things through Christ who strengthens me" (Phil. 4:13).

About the Author

Joe Nathan Hill currently lives in Birmingham, Alabama, enjoying retirement. He is learning to play the guitar. He spends time with his grandchildren and goes hunting and fishing as often as he can. He thanks God that he successfully recovered from several serious illnesses and continues to have a positive outlook on life.

CPSIA information can be obtained
at www.ICGtesting.com
Printed in the USA
BVHW080743200122
626620BV00006B/397